*In this book, I will take you through
Birthing Floor, a place of prayer a
and help you discover that which you have inside
of you that you don't know about. You are about
to give birth to what God has placed inside of you,
your dreams are about to become reality.*

Blessings — Robin J Dinnanauth

Therefore, if anyone is in Christ, he is a new creation; the old has gone, the new has come!
2 Corinthians 5:17

THE BIRTHING FLOOR

"THE THINGS YOU CAN'T SEE ARE MORE POWERFUL THAN THE THINGS YOU CAN SEE".

Robin Dinnanauth
An Ambassador of Jesus Christ

Copyright © 2010 by Robin Dinnanauth

Birthing Floor
A place of Spiritual Warfare Prayer and Intercession
By Robin Dinnanauth

Printed in the United States of America

Library of Congress Cataloging-in-Publication Data
ISBN 9781612154428

All rights reserved solely by the author. The author guarantees all contents are original and do not infringe upon the legal rights of any other person or work. No part of this book may be reproduced in any form without the permission of the author. The views expressed in this book are not necessarily those of the publisher.

Unless otherwise indicated, Bible quotations are taken from The Amplified® Bible. Copyright © 1954, 1958, 1962, 1964, 1965, 1987 by The Lockman Foundation Used by permission." (www.Lockman.org)

www.xulonpress.com

This book is dedicated to every person who acknowledged Jesus Christ as personal Lord and Savior and who wants to discover their true potentials, purpose and destiny in Christ, who has called them out of darkness into his marvelous light.

CONTENTS

ACKNOWLEDGMENT	ix
ABOUT THE AUTHOR	xi
PREFACE	The Birthing Floor - A Place of Prayer and Intercession ... xiii
INTRODUCTION	A Journey of Endurance & Promise ... xxv
CHAPTER ONE	The Birthing Process of Vision ... 19
CHAPTER TWO	Conception and the Birthing of Destiny ... 28
CHAPTER THREE	The Birthing of Purpose & Possibilities ... 41
CHAPTER FOUR	The Birthing of spiritual journey to meet with God ... 60
CHAPTER FIVE	The Birthing of Passionate Prayer ... 75
CHAPTER SIX	The place of Consecration ... 88
CHAPTER SEVEN	The place to Experience God's Glory ... 100
CHAPTER EIGHT	The Birthing of Breakthrough ... 112

CHATPER NINE   Breaking forth to birthing the New Me . . 120

CHAPTER TEN   Birthing of Freedom – Declaration 127

placed inside of you. Go after your dreams because your dreams will never come after you.

To the dedicated, God-fearing and hardworking staff and Volunteer of the Robin Healing Ministries: Thank you for your hard work, I would like to say special thanks to all of you for understanding me especially in my difficult and trying times. Thanks to Brother Rovin Gajadar, Sister Maitree Haridin and Sister Nickasie Califia Niles for your faithful dedication in our offices. Special thanks to Rev. Aldwyn Williams for editing this book and for your continued support and prayers in all my projects.

To Rev. Mohendra Ramsarup, Rev. Roger Hans, Brother Reggie Dinnanauth and Elder Ishry Singh who always stood with me and encouraged me in difficult times. Thanks to the support staff and volunteer of the Birthing Floor team: Brother George Narine, Sister Monica Ramoutar, Elder Gloria Marksman, my armor bearer Steven Mootoo and my faithful mother Silvee Dinnanauth who always looked out for my interest.

I would like to say special thanks to Xulon press and the entire production teams, thank you very much for believing in me and to publish all of my books.

ACKNOWLEDGEMENTS

With a grateful heart I would like to say special thanks to some very important people in my life who have helped me tremendously.

First to my personal Lord and savior Jesus Christ, who is our soon coming King! Thank you for entrusting me with the healing and deliverance anointing and for placing some very special people in my life that has helped me through my birthing process.

To my inspiration and beautiful wife Veronica, who stood by my side and with strength and continued support for the past fourteen years. Veronica has been my prayer warrior, my best friend and most important my faithful partner who is always there to encourage me to go on and finish whatever I am doing. Veronica is a great woman of God and I love her with my every being. To you my loving wife: it's a miracle how we first met and it continued to be a miracle as God continued to keep us together as we continue to work to build his kingdom. I love you and thank you for standing by my side and for your total dedication and help while I was writing this book.

To my gifted and God-given children Justin M., Josiah Timothy and Jaden Luke, thank you for giving me the time to write this book and understand me when I needed some quiet time alone. I would like to specially dedicate this book to the three of you. Other than Jesus Christ my personal Lord and Savior the three of you are my joy, inspiration and blessings. Your mom and I love you and pray God's richest blessing on your lives. Always remember that in God's perfect timing allow him to conceive you with his purpose and destiny and follow his will so that you all can birth that which God has placed inside of you. Go after your dreams because your dreams will never come after you.

To the dedicated, God-fearing and hardworking staff and Volunteer of the Robin Healing Ministries: Thank you for your hard work, I would like to say special thanks to all of you for understanding me especially in my difficult and trying times. Thanks to Brother Rovin Gajadar, Sister Maitree Haridin and Sister Nickasie Califia Niles for your faithful dedication in our offices. Special thanks to Rev. Aldwyn Williams for editing this book and for your continued support and prayers in all my projects.

To Rev. Mohendra Ramsarup, Rev. Roger Hans, Brother Reggie Dinnanauth and Elder Ishry Singh who always stood with me and encouraged me in difficult times. Thanks to the support staff and volunteer of the Birthing Floor team: Brother George Narine, Sister Monica Ramoutar, Elder Gloria Marksman, my armor bearer Steven Mootoo and my faithful mother Silvee Dinnanauth who always looked out for my interest.

I would like to say special thanks to Xulon press and the entire production teams, thank you very much for believing in me and to publish all of my books.

ABOUT THE AUTHOR

Robin Dinnanauth is an active Revivalist ministering the Gospel of the Lord Jesus Christ, demonstrating God's Miraculous Saving, Healing and Deliverance power in the United States of America and around the World. He has been used mightily by God flowing in the ministry gift of Healing and Deliverance, preaching in Crusades, Conferences and Revival meetings. He is out in front battling Satan, leading the charge against demonic forces that appear to have so many souls in torment. He is also the Author of "Every Day with Jesus", "Miracles Still Happen" and bestselling Book "Let the Warfare Begin."

As a highly sought-after crusader and revival speaker who God has raised up as a prophetic voice to the world, Robin is calling people to Jesus Christ through the good news of the Gospel and the power of the blood of the Lamb. Thousands experience the saving, healing and deliverance message of Jesus Christ as he ministers hope to the sick, the afflicted and the hurting.

He is known for his dynamic and anointed Spiritual Warfare Prayer, Healing and Deliverance Ministry and as an ordained Minister, Pastor, Overseer, and Sought-after conference speaker. He is the founder of the Emmanuel Full Gospel Assemblies of Churches, Emmanuel Full Gospel Assemblies Ministerial Fellowship, Emmanuel Bible Training Institute, Robin Healing Ministries and the Birthing Floor Conference.

PREFACE

THE BIRTHING FLOOR A PLACE OF PRAYER AND INTERCESSION

As I look back at my life where I was and where I am today and looking into where God is taking me, I realized that I have something within me that needs to come forth and birth me into my future success and take me to the place where God himself wants me to be. So that makes me now a thinker and no longer a self dream killer.

I realized in the realm of the Spirit that I was my own hindrance in life, just because I wanted people to tell me who I am and what I should do and where I should go and when to start bringing forth my fruits. But that concept has now changed when I discovered the Birthing Floor, a place of prayer and personal intercession, a place where I can enter in to give birth to my destiny and walk in a different realm because God's word declares that we can approach his throne of grace. Hebrews 4:16 says Let us then fearlessly and confidently and boldly draw near to the throne of grace (the throne of God's unmerited favor to us sinners), that we may receive mercy [for our failures] and find grace to help in good times for every need [appropriate help and well-timed help, coming just when we need it].

After carefully examining some of the great men and women of the Bible who had struggle in their lives and how they used the anointing and the greatness that is within them to break out of their issues and situations, I finally come to a place in my life where

I can now reflect on some of the process they used and apply it to my own life for my personal breakthrough.

Stop and reflect on some of those men and women in Jesus' Genealogy who broke through to the Birthing floor – A place of Destiny. You can do the same today with your life; you can get yourself to the spiritual birthing floor "a place of prayer and intercession and deliver that which God has placed inside of you.

In this book the Birthing Floor, I will take you through the Journey to the Birthing Floor and help you discover that which you have inside of you that you don't know about. Always remember **"THE THINGS YOU CAN'T SEE ARE MORE POWERFUL THAN THE THINGS YOU CAN SEE"**.

There is so much hidden treasures inside of you that need to be birthed out and only you can give birth to that which is inside of you. The word of God says "I have strength for all things in Christ Who empowers me, I am ready for anything and equal to anything through Him who infuses inner strength into me; I am self-sufficient in Christ's sufficiency. Philippians 4:13 (Amplified Bible)

Did you ever ask yourself this question – Where does God want me and what can I do with the very strength that God has given me? Well let me help you with the answer and that is the Birthing Floor. A place of sanctification, a place of consecration, a place of purification, a place of justification, a place of regeneration, a place where you can position yourself for the out-pouring of the spirit of God and a place of prosperity so that you can walk into your destiny.

There is a clarion call; God is saying to his bride "So, come out from among (unbelievers), and separate (sever) yourselves from them, says the Lord, and touch not (any) unclean thing; then I will receive you kindly and treat you with favor. 2 Corinthians 6:17 Amplified Version.

Stop letting people hold you back from giving birth to your dreams, your vision and your destiny. Let that which is inside of you come forth and be birthed out, give birth to that business, give birth to that ministry, give birth to your healing, give birth to that desire of yours, you have been conceived by the Holy Spirit with that which you are carrying. Come to the Birthing Floor, position yourself for the pouring and give birth in the realm of the spirit now.

INTRODUCTION

A Journey of Endurance & Promise

There is a Promise that God has promised from the beginning of time and that is to be fruitful and multiply. He has impregnated you with a promise of multiplication, and given you the choice to journey with such a blessing and success to give birth to that which he has impregnated you with but many people has been side tracked by the Abortionist-Satan who has been distracting humanity and taking them out of alignment from their destiny so that he can force abortion. What Satan wants is to abort the power and authority that God has placed inside of every believer of Christ. Satan knows the greatness that lies within every born again Christian, so he is afraid of your greatness as a chosen vessel of God.

God has placed inside of you dreams, visions and ideas of how to get wealth, how to walk into your destiny, how to be an over-comer, how stay in alignment and be happy, how to live a stress free life, how to enjoy the goodness of him who called you out of darkness into his marvelous light, how to stay healed and delivered, how to seek him first and the list can go on and on but the Abortionist-Satan because he knows what God has placed inside of you, he is afraid of what's going to come out of you. Satan knows that God's hands are upon your life and you are getting stronger everyday as you discover the goodness of God in your life. Satan knows that you have learnt how to become an overcomer and trust God for your healing, deliverance, breakthrough and every other blessing in your life so he is making plans to destroy the trust and confidence you have in Christ. But it is time for you to stand firm and let him know that he should have had done it when he had you but now it's too late because you have discovered your birthing floor a place of giving birth to your greatness. It's time now for you to let Satan know he can't get you now because he has lost his opportunity and it's too late because you are covered under the blood of Jesus Christ, and you can only say this because you discovered how to hear from God and how to communicate with him because you are now identifying your personal birthing floor through prayer and intercession.

Whenever you are in prayer and intercession, there is always God's supernatural covering over you, no devil or human can touch you. God will put fear in the heart of those who want to hurt you or even want to destroy that which you have inside you. Exodus 1:15-16 says And the king of Egypt spake to the Hebrew midwives, of which the name of the one was Shiphrah, and the name of the other Puah: And he said, When ye do the office of a midwife to the Hebrew women, and see them upon the stools; if it be a son, then ye shall kill him: but if it be a daughter, then she shall live.

God's covering was on the children of Israel and he heard the cry of Israel and promised to deliver them out of Egypt, so he decided to place a deliverer in the midst of them. And Pharaoh, the then king of Egypt discovers that Israel was pregnant with a deliverer, so he instructed the midwives to kill every male child that was going to be born of the Israelites women. I want you to know that Satan knows what you have inside of you and he will do everything possible just to kill it because he just discovered that you are getting stronger, but always remember you have a promise. I can clearly remember when God spoke to me and said Robin I will take you to preach the Gospel to the nations around the world. And as I looked at myself it seems so impossible, talking to myself how can this be when I have no money, I don't know anyone how can this really be; but God reminds me that he is a God of promise and will make every impossible situation possible. If he could have done it for Joseph then he can do it for you.

Birthing Floor

The Abortionist-Satan loves to put doubt in our hearts especially when it comes to the promises of God and whenever he can't have us to doubt God he then tries to put fear in our hearts so that he can help us to abort the promises of God in our lives. You see here Satan the abortionist wants to abort the promise that Israel had but God stepped right in and put fear in the lives of the midwives. God is saying endure your suffering and keep looking up to him, who is the author and finisher of your faith and journey yourself to the birthing floor a place of prayer supplication and intercession because he is about to bring to pass that which he has said and will allow you to bring forth that which he has promised. You must understand that your promises are locked up inside of you. God has conceived every blessing he has in store for you inside of you.

God has been moving mightily in the realm of the Sprit and is speaking to his people in such a time as this by calling back his chosen people into alignment and placed them back on this journey to realize that he is the God who has made the heaven and the earth. And he is that God who has given man dominion over the earth.

According to the book of Genesis 1:26-28: God said, Let Us [Father, Son, and Holy Spirit] make mankind in Our image, after Our likeness, and let them have complete authority over the fish of the sea, the birds of the air, the [tame] beasts, and over all of the earth, and over everything that creeps upon the earth.

So God created man in His own image, in the image and likeness of God He created him; male and female He created them.

And God blessed them and said to them, Be fruitful, multiply, and fill the earth, and subdue it [using all its vast resources in the service of God and man]; and have dominion over the fish of the sea, the birds of the air, and over every living creature that moves upon the earth.

And God said, See, I have given you every plant yielding seed that is on the face of all the land and every tree with seed in its fruit; you shall have them for food.

And to all the animals on the earth and to every bird of the air and to everything that creeps on the ground—to everything in which there is the breath of life—I have given every green plant for food. And it was so.

God has designed us to be reproductive according to his word in Genesis 1:28. He has placed in us true wealth according to his word. There are dreams, visions and ideas that are locked up inside of you that God himself has conceived and placed in you. But you have to give birth to that which is inside of you so that you can be successful and prosperous. How can you be successful and prosperous if you don't first give birth to that which God has placed inside of you?

CHAPTER ONE

THE BIRTHING PROCESS OF VISION

Where there is no vision [no redemptive revelation of God], the people perish; but he who keeps the law [of God, which includes that of man]—blessed (happy, fortunate, and enviable) is he. Proverbs 29:18

God has placed a mandate upon my heart to conduct seventy days of revival called the Birthing Floor and this revival has inspired me to write this book called the birthing floor. And this is because he placed a vision in my spirit and caused me to birth it out. God wants to birth in your spirit a vision and then bring you to a place of birthing.

The bible says in Proverbs 29:18 Where there is no vision [no redemptive revelation of God], the people perish; but he who keeps the law [of God, which includes that of man]—blessed (happy, fortunate, and enviable) is he. "The vision to which this verse refers is spiritual vision.

Spiritual vision will provide direction for your life. It provides challenge and structure for you. Without it, you become spiritually dead. Developing spiritual vision is the process of recognizing the purpose for which you have been brought into the Kingdom of God. Now you may ask why is a spiritual vision necessary for me? How will I perish without it? These are great questions and the answer can be found in many Biblical examples.

Look at the Prophet Elisha and his servant, Gehazi. According to 11 Kings 6:15-17 says ¹⁵When the servant of the man of God rose early and went out, behold, an army with horses and chariots was around the city. Elisha's servant said to him, Alas, my master! What shall we do?

¹⁶[Elisha] answered, Fear not; for those with us are more than those with them. ¹⁷Then Elisha prayed, Lord, I pray You, open his eyes that he may see. And the Lord opened the young man's eyes, and he saw, and behold, the mountain was full of horses and chariots of fire round about Elisha.

God's people, Israel, were surrounded by the enemy nation of Syria. There were many soldiers, horses, and chariots of war. When Elisha's servant, Gehazi, saw the great force of the enemy he was afraid. He cried out to Elisha, "What shall we do?" Elisha told him: *"Fear not, for they that be with us are more than they that be with them."*

Elisha prayed that God would open Gehazi's eyes and allow him to see in the spirit world. The request was granted, and Gehazi saw the spiritual forces of God surrounding Israel. In this example, God actually let Gehazi see the spiritual vision with his natural eyes. But the important point is that without spiritual vision you cannot see beyond the natural circumstances of life. Like Gehazi, they are defeated by the powers of the enemy which they see at work in the natural world around them. Their vision is focused on their problems and their lives become a cycle of crying out, "What shall we do?" Without spiritual vision, they cannot see and understand the divine plan of God.

Before you were born again you were blinded by sin and through salvation by the blood of Jesus your basic blindness is healed and God placed within you his Spirit which is the Holy Spirit and a Vision. Then God wants to develop your spiritual vision through the Holy Spirit. This process is a spiritual parallel of an actual incident in the ministry of Jesus: According to Mark 8:22-25 And they came to Bethsaida. And [people] brought to Him a blind man and begged Him to touch him.

²³And He caught the blind man by the hand and led him out of the village; and when He had spit on his eyes and put His hands upon him, He asked him, Do you [possibly] see anything? ²⁴And he looked up and said, I see people, but [they look] like trees, walking.

²⁵Then He put His hands on his eyes again; and the man looked intently [that is, fixed his eyes on definite objects], and he was restored and saw everything distinctly [even what was at a distance].

This miracle was an actual physical healing performed by Jesus during His earthly ministry. Why didn't the first touch of Jesus heal the man completely? Didn't Jesus have all power? Wasn't He the Son of the living God? Jesus was providing a natural example of a spiritual truth. Jesus wants to touch you spiritually just as He did in this natural healing. First He wants to clear up the basic blindness of sin in your life. Then He wants to develop your spiritual vision.

Spiritual vision involves seeing beyond the natural world into the spiritual world. It is understanding the divine purpose of God and recognizing your part in His plan. If you find yourself spiritually "perishing" then you will find yourself in one of the following categories:

- You will not have spiritual vision.
- You will receive a spiritual vision but you will be disobedient to it.
- You will have a vision, but do not know how to fulfill it. You tried and failed or perhaps have never tried at all.

Spiritual vision will provides a clear image of what God wants you to birth out and then directs every step of your life towards achieving that goal. The Apostle Paul had spiritual vision. He said: in the book of Acts 26:19 Wherefore, O King Agrippa, I was not disobedient unto the heavenly vision,

The heavenly [spiritual] vision became the compelling force in Paul's life. He recognized that having a vision is not enough. Action must be taken to achieve the vision. A vision can remain "visionary."

This means it never becomes a reality because you never acted on it.

When God gives a vision He also provides spiritual and practical strategies for fulfilling it. When God gave Paul a spiritual vision, He gave him specific things to do to fulfill the vision. In Acts 26:16-18 But arise and stand upon your feet; for I have appeared to you for this purpose, that I might appoint you to serve as [My] minister and to bear witness both to what you have seen of Me and to that in which I will appear to you, [17]Choosing you out [selecting you for Myself] and delivering you from among this [Jewish] people and the Gentiles to whom I am sending you [18]To open their eyes that they may turn from darkness to light and from the power of Satan to God, so that they may thus receive forgiveness and release from their sins and a place and portion among those who are consecrated and purified by faith in Me.

God wants to give you a spiritual vision for the purpose of making you the person you desire to be according to his will and purpose. God wants to give you objectives [a plan] to achieve the vision. If you look at the Apostle Paul, his vision that God gave him was to bring salvation to the gentiles. He was to: Open their spiritual eyes from darkness to light turn them from the power of Satan to God. Lead them to forgiveness of sins, reveal their spiritual inheritance made possible by faith. What is your vision?

God wants to give you a spiritual vision just as He did Paul. God also wants to reveal the purposes and objectives which will enable you to fulfill the vision. As you experience the "birth of a vision" you will become a participator instead of a mere spectator in God's divine plan. The natural birth process which brings a human baby into the world is similar to the process of the birth of a vision in the spirit world. You will experience the following stages as you give birth to spiritual vision.

CONCEPTION: "Conception" means to create. A spiritual vision of destiny is created in your spirit by God. When God gave Paul spiritual vision He identified the source. He said, "I am Jesus" in Acts 26:15. God conceived Paul's vision. Whenever God himself conceived you with something it will last forever and he will identify the source. It is very important to ask God to conceive within you that which you desire. Don't you ever try to conceive your destiny by yourself it will never prosper. Allow God himself to do it for you and it will be successful. Many people started ministry, business, studies etc without God's direction. And because it wasn't the will or plan of God it failed, died or withered away. Allow God to create your path. The word of God says Psalm 37:23 the steps of a [good] man are directed and established by the Lord when He delights in his way [and He busies Himself with his every step].

DEVELOPMENT: When God first gave you a spiritual vision and birth destiny in you, it is in "embryo" form. An embryo is a basic cell of life. Just like the development of the human embryo, God develops your spiritual vision and destiny as you grow in Him. The basic cell of life in the human baby is the embryo; from it all the basic human features are developed. If you try to change the embryo, deformity or death can occur to the child. During the development stages of your destiny it is very important to stay under the covering of God anointing and study the word of God, seek him in fasting and prayer for guidance and tune your ears to hear from the throne room of God.

God conceives the basic spiritual vision and destiny within you. The vision and destiny must remain the embryo from which all features develop. If you try to change the vision or destiny, it will be deformed from the perfect plan of God, or it may be aborted. When the vision and destiny is conceived by God in your spirit it must always remain the same although you may fulfill it in different ways.

The vision will grow and develop as you mature spiritually. Its features will not be the same as yesterday, last week, or last month. But you must never forget the basic vision which is the divine purpose for which you are called. This development of a vision will be a stretching experience as it is in the natural world within the body of a mother. If the vision does not develop within you it will die. Just as a mother carries her child within her body, when you receive this vision it is with you constantly. It becomes a vital, living part of you.

It draws from your own life source as well as from the divine source which conceived it.

While the baby is developing, a pregnant mother will deny herself of certain things. As your spiritual vision develops, you may have to do this also. You may have to deny yourself of your own plans and ambitions. You may have to lay aside worldly treasures. You will have to sacrifice time to fast and pray.

TRAVAIL: According to the book of Ecclesiastes 5:3 it says For a dream comes with much business and painful effort, and a fool's voice with many words. The meaning of the word "multitude" is great. "Business", according to one Hebrew meaning, is travail [difficulty]. So a dream or vision comes through "great travail." In natural birth there are facts about travail that parallel the spiritual travail which births a vision. Natural travail is a time of intense, concentrated effort to birth the child. This time of travail is also called "labor." As in the delivery of a child, a spiritual vision is birthed by intense mental, physical, and spiritual concentration. It is important that you concentrate on what God wants to birth in your spirit. Because whatever God birth in your spirit is what will come out of you.

In the natural world during labor [travail], the one giving birth must let the natural forces take control. Physically forcing the child into the birth canal before it opens can kill the child. The same is true in the spirit world. Let God take control of your life. If you try to birth the vision in your own strength it will abort the plan of God. Everything within you may cry out to push and bring the spiritual vision forth with natural abilities. But by self-effort you can destroy the vision. Peter cried out to Christ, "Depart from me, for I am a sinful man," when he realized what Christ was calling him to do according to Luke 5:8. He knew the vision was too great for him to fulfill by his natural strength and abilities. As a mother in travail hides herself from public gaze, so those in travail spiritually must be alone with God.

THE TIME OF TRANSITION: In the natural birth process there is a time during labor known as the time of "transition." It is the most difficult time of travail right before the birth canal is open to permit the birth of the child. This parallels the birth of a vision in the spirit world. When God births in you a spiritual vision and placed destiny inside of you; you will experience a time of transition. Transition means change. As God gives you this spiritual vision it is going to require change in your life. It will call for new commitment and dedication. You may experience pressure in every area of your life. Everything within you may cry out for relief from the spiritual birth pangs of what God is bringing forth. This is the point where many fail to receive the vision. Time and time again God has brought His people to the time of transition to birth His vision within them.

But because the transition was too difficult many have turned back. They could not take the pressure of this most difficult time. It required changes in their thought patterns and lifestyle which they were not willing to make. They could not abandon self-effort and tradition. They could not set aside their own ambitions and desires to embrace the plan of God. This is what happened to the nation of Israel: According to Isaiah 26:17-18 the bible says As a woman with child drawing near the time of her delivery is in pain and writhes and cries out in her pangs, so we have been before You (at Your presence), O Lord. [18]We have been with child, we have been writhing and in pain; we have, as it were, brought forth [only] wind. We have not wrought any deliverance in the earth, and the inhabitants of the world [of Israel] have not yet been born.

Travail brings sorrow but it leads to the birth which brings joy: The bible says A woman when she is in travail hath sorrow, because her hour is come: but as soon as she is delivered of the child, she remembereth no more the anguish, for joy that a man is born into the world. John 16:21. We are told in Isaiah 53:11 that God witnessed the travail of Jesus Christ and was satisfied. A vision was fulfilled that day on Calvary it was a vision that had been promised since the fall of man into sin according to Genesis 3:15. Through travail, the vision of redemption from sin became a reality.

Travail is a painful experience, but it is only through travail that the vision can be birthed: the bible says for as soon as Zion travailed, she brought forth her children. Shall I bring to the birth, and not cause to bring forth? saith the Lord: shall I cause to bring forth, and shut the womb? saith thy God according to Isaiah 66:8-9.

The development of a spiritual vision has an expected end, just as a human embryo. That end is birth. Prematurity of birth and delay of birth can result in death, both in the natural birth process and in the birth of spiritual vision. After birth in the natural world the child continues to grow and develop. After the birth of this spiritual vision it will continue to grow and develop. It will have new features and form, but they all must develop from that basic cell of spiritual life which is the vision.

Abraham tried to bring forth his God-given vision through self-effort by the birth of Ishmael. He knew God wanted to make him a great nation and he thought an heir could not come through his wife, Sarah. So he did something about it and Ishmael was born. But whose power was behind Ishmael, that of Abraham or that of God? Was the fulfillment of the vision through Ishmael manmade or God-made? You can bring an Ishmael on the scene through your own efforts. Ishmael represents your plans and methods of trying to do God's will through natural abilities. But the heavenly vision, represented by Isaac, must be birthed by God. Who is the source of spiritual vision? When asked, "What shall we do, that we might work the works of God?" Jesus responded, "This is the work of God", indicating that He, Himself, was the source according to John 6:28-29.

God did not want Abraham to be the source of the heavenly vision any more than He wants us to bring forth man-made or organizationally-made visions. God is the source of spiritual vision. The vision for your destiny which you will receive after reading this book is Gods plan. It is not a plan of man, a denomination, or an organization. Scripture has no record of God speaking again to Abraham for thirteen years after the birth of Ishmael. Not until it was humanly impossible for Abraham to have a child did God again stir the vision within him. By then, self-effort had died. Then came the birth of a vision, for in the perfect timing of God Isaac was miraculously born. But with the birth of God's plan [Isaac], Ishmael [self-effort] must be cast out.

It is time for your Isaac [God's plan] to be birthed in your spirit. In order for this to happen, Ishmael must be cast out. It is a painful experience to cast out self-effort, your plans, ambitions, tradition, and organizational programs. But God is saying to you as He did to Abraham, "Grieve not for Ishmael [self-effort], for in Isaac shall your seed be called." In Isaac the source of the vision was God.

ARE YOU READY? Birth requires change. In the natural world, the child must leave the security of the womb. When you were born again you had to leave the old life of sin. You had to let Jesus change your thought and action patterns. To give birth to spiritual vision, purpose and destiny it also requires change. It requires courage to step from the known into the unknown. Are you ready to receive that spiritual vision, purpose and destiny? Are you willing to experience spiritual travail in order to birth something new and vital in your life? If you are not willing you had better stop what you are doing and get down to serious prayer at the birthing floor and get serious with your life. Once you discover your vision at the birthing floor and give birth to it, then your life will never again be the same.

CHAPTER TWO

CONCEPTION & THE BIRTHING OF DESTINY

Get in Position - You are about to conceive with Destiny

You shall not need to fight in this battle; take your positions, stand still, and see the deliverance of the Lord [Who is] with you, O Judah and Jerusalem. Fear not nor be dismayed. Tomorrow go out against them, for the Lord is with you. 2 Chronicles 20:17 (Amplified Bible)

God has created every one with a plan and purpose, and he expects you to fulfill his plan and purpose in your lives. You were created not to be used or manipulated by man but to be used by Him and him only. There are times when you probably will remember that you actually allow people to determine your destiny or wants people to notice or identify and recognize you when you discover your talent and strength or tell sometime you want people to tell you who we are, when God is trying to say hello, hello can you hear me, hello, I know who you are, I know you by name because I am the one that form you even from your mother's womb. In the book of Jeremiah 1:4-10 the bible says: Then the word of the Lord came to me [Jeremiah], saying,

Before I formed you in the womb I knew [and] approved of you [as My chosen instrument], and before you were born I separated and set you apart, consecrating you; [and] I appointed you as a prophet to the nations.

Then said I, Ah, Lord God! Behold, I cannot speak, for I am only a youth. But the Lord said to me, Say not, I am only a youth; for you shall go to all to whom I shall send you, and whatever I command you, you shall speak. Be not afraid of them [their faces], for I am with you to deliver you, says the Lord.

Then the Lord put forth His hand and touched my mouth. And the Lord said to me, Behold, I have put my words in your mouth. See, I have this day appointed you to the oversight of the nations and of the kingdoms to root out and pull down, to destroy and to overthrow, to build and to plant.

You can go ahead and meditate on what God has spoken to the prophet Jeremiah, according to the scripture above, here is where God has placed within Jeremiah the prophetic ministry and has positioned him as a prophet. He was spiritually pregnant with the prophetic unction. But Jeremiah did not recognize what he was carrying within him until God had spoken to him. God told the prophet Jeremiah that he knew him from his mother womb and secondly he told him that he was ordained as a prophet to set over nations, over kingdoms, to root out, and to pull down and to destroy and to throw down to build and to plant.

So if you carefully examine this scripture and see yourself fitted in there then that is what God is saying to you today. There is something greater that is locked up inside of you that is full of destiny that you did not discover as yet. God has impregnated you with a desire to fulfill your destiny for a long time now, so its time now for you to discover that which is inside of you and birth it out. And when you can discover what is inside of you and ready to birth it out, God will prepare somebody to help you in the process.

The bible says in 1 Samuel 9:1-2 there was a wealthy, influential man named Kish from the tribe of Benjamin. He was the son of Abiel, son of Zeror, son of Becorath, son of Aphiah, of the tribe of Benjamin. His son Saul was the most handsome man in Israel—head and shoulders taller than anyone else in the land. Also look at 1 Samuel 9:15-17. Now the LORD had told Samuel in his ear a day before Saul came, saying, To morrow about this time I will send thee a man out of the land of Benjamin, and thou shalt anoint him to be captain over my people Israel, that he may save my people out of the hand of the Philistines: for I have looked upon my people, because their cry is come unto me. And when Samuel saw Saul, the LORD said unto him, Behold the man whom I spake to thee of! This same shall reign over my people.

Now you can also read 1 Samuel 10:6 it says at that time the Spirit of the LORD will come powerfully upon you, and you will prophesy with them. You will be changed into a different person. And verse 9 of I Samuel 10 says As Saul turned and started to leave, God gave him a new heart, and all Samuel's signs were fulfilled that day. And in verse 7 of I Samuel 7 for God is with thee.

As you read all these verses it shows you that the prophet Samuel did not choose Saul (per say) nor did the children of Israel choose Saul to lead them out of the bondage of the Philistines, but rather God chose this man. Not as some after thought or by mistake, but this was the man that God had chosen.

The Lord chose him, anointed him, gave him another heart, and went with him. In essence what the Lord was telling Samuel, "Take a good look" Samuel, This is the man I have chosen, this is the man who will do the job, this is the man that has been blessed with a destiny, and purpose, and a future. So it is time to fulfill your destiny. You have been called for such a time as this, you have been chosen, you have been given a job to do, not by man or by mistake, but by God, so fulfill your destiny.

Now if you are asking the question. "What is "Destiny"? In simple terms, Destiny is God's purpose for you. It is your appointed and ordained future. Destiny is what God has predetermined for you to become, it is his divine will for your existence.

It can be so sad at times to read within the scripture and that even people who experience God's glory have missed their destiny. They have aborted the plan, and the will of God for their lives, they started out right, had a great desire, but somewhere along the way they got sidetracked and missed out on their destiny.

It is time that you take a look at where you are and what are you doing, just to make sure you are in alignment with God and keep asking yourself this question, Am I ready to fulfill my destiny? Or Am I walking in my Destiny?

If you look at Saul he was a man that missed his opportunity, God himself chose Saul to lead his people out of bondage. When the prophet Samuel first laid eyes on Saul, the Lord said, "...Behold this is the man that I have chosen, he will be the one to lead my people, and reign over them. An anointed man and man that at one time were led by the Spirit of the Lord, he was gifted with a spirit of prophecy, destined by God to lead Israel — and God was with him. He was a man with a destiny, he was a mighty man of valor, he was a great warrior, he feared God, and he loved God. That's why God chose him but yet one of the most tragic pictures you can see within this story is when, Saul, the king of Israel began to fall apart. He only walked in his destiny for a while. He started off right, but somewhere along the way got tripped up.

He got within himself and instead of trying to fulfill his destiny, he started desiring the applause of the people, he began to compromise the plan, and will of God. And the plan of God was to lead God's people out of bondage.

It is very important to know that you have not been called to compromise the message God gave you, also you cannot compromise your mission as a believer, you must try and bring the Lost to the Cross.

If you notice in the life of Saul, when he was coming to the end of his life, how he was faced with one of his biggest battle of his life, but his heart now was filled with fear. I Samuel 28:15 say "Why have you disturbed me by calling me back?" Samuel asked Saul. "Because I am in deep trouble," Saul replied. "The Philistines are at war with me, and God has left me and won't reply by prophets or dreams. So I have called for you to tell me what to do."

By his own admission, the Lord had left him, and now his heart was filled with fear, because he chose rather to please the people, rather than please God, and trust God. Keep in mind that the coming of Jesus Christ is near, you may be the generation that will see him come in the clouds of glory, and now that you are at the end of the race, there is no time to compromise your principles but to fulfill your purpose with God.

My heart is not filled with fear, and worry, and confusion, God has not forsaken us as some might believe, but I understand that my life and your life has been filled with destiny. You have purpose, you have a Destiny and God wants you to understand your destiny. All throughout the bible there were Kings, and Priests, and Prophets, and Saints, and Servants, Worshippers, and Shepherds, and Tentmakers, that had destinies to fulfill.

And all throughout the scripture there are lessons for you to learn. And that most important lesson for you to learn is that you cannot compare your destiny to theirs. What God did for them in times of old was for them, but I believe that God wants to do something fresh for you, something new. In the book of Isaiah 43:18-19 say "But forget all that it is nothing compared to what I am going to do. For I am about to do something new. See, I have already begun! Do you not see it? I will make a pathway through the wilderness. I will create rivers in the dry wasteland.

And in the book of Joel 2:28-29 The bible says "Then, after doing all those things, I will pour out my Spirit upon all people. Your sons and daughters will prophesy. Your old men will dream dreams, and your young men will see visions. In those days I will pour out my Spirit even on servants—men and women alike.

God will not judge this generation, by what our forefathers did. Their lives have nothing to do with our destiny; they will have their just reward. But our generation will be judged by what we have been given, and what we have done with what we have been given.

You are living in a generation that wants to make all kinds of excuses; you want to blame everyone else for your struggles. You want to use for and excuse as a believer, that you are living in a wicked society. This is your time, this is your chance; this is your opportunity fulfill your destiny. Quit making excuses, quit waiting for a more convenient time, you have no other time, and you have a destiny to fulfill. The book of Romans 13:11 say this is all the more urgent, for you know how late it is; time is running out. Wake up, for our salvation is nearer now than when we first believed.

You see the devil doesn't care how much you do for God, as long as you don't do it today. It is his job to get you to pass up your opportunity; to lose your chance, and to give up on your destiny.

But you have been given a mandate by God through his word to work while it is yet day for night cometh and no man can work. As Jesus said; As long as I am in the world, I am the light of the world.

You have the Holy Ghost, you have the message, you have the anointing, and you have the power. Paul said in; 2 Corinthians 4:7-9 We now have this light shining in our hearts, but we ourselves are like fragile clay jars containing this great treasure. This makes it clear that our great power is from God, not from ourselves. We are pressed on every side by troubles, but we are not crushed. We are perplexed, but not driven to despair. We are hunted down, but never abandoned by God. We get knocked down, but we are not destroyed.

You have to believe that where you need to get as a believer, is to understand that you don't have time any longer to have our own personal destinies, it time you come together within yourself, as a mighty champion, and understand you have a job to do and that is to work toward fulfilling the mandate that God has placed within you.

Listen to what God is telling you, in essence in the last days, or if you please in the fullness of time, I have given you a purpose. And that is to come into the adoption of Jesus Christ, to live blameless, to praise and glorify my name. Why because I have predestined you according to my purpose, to praise and glorify my name.

Your destiny is to be an adopted child of God! You have been adopted by the heavenly Father and the devil no longer has any claim on us. Always remember that a person's destiny is not measured by his great works, his achievements and exploits but his/her special accomplishments.

God is not requiring some great accomplishment from us. The bible says in Micah 6:8 No, O people, the LORD has told you what is good, and this is what he requires of you: to do what is right, to love mercy, and to walk humbly with your God.

God has a destiny for you, and we will not find that destiny through the natural eye. It will come by a heavenly vision. So as you get down to the birthing floor you will able to see it through your spiritual eyes. When you see in the spirit you will have vision. In Proverbs 29:18 the bible says where there is no vision, the people perish. The purpose of vision is to give direction, and guidance, and insight into the will of God. Vision is something that addresses the future, and is not swayed by the today, it will not be changed by circumstances around it or by the obstacles that will try to detour it, but it is something directed by God to give purpose and direction for the future.

When we as children of God understand that we have a destiny and that God has called and chosen you, and anointed you, to run this race, and to fight this fight and you begin to follow the destiny that has been laid out there for you then you as the believer will truly know that you have fulfilled your purpose and is walking in your destiny.

Paul said; forget those things which are behind, and reaching forth unto those things which are before, press toward the mark for the prize of the high calling of God in Christ Jesus. In Hebrew 12:2 say we do this by keeping our eyes on Jesus, the champion who initiates and perfects our faith. Because of the joy awaiting him, he endured the cross, disregarding its shame. Now he is seated in the place of honor beside God's throne.

How could Jesus endure that cross? He saw what was on the other side of the cross, he understood his destiny, and purpose. He saw down through the annals of time an saw you as an individual who is full of purpose and destiny.

God understood that destiny was a good place for dreams, and he also understood that the future far exceeds the accomplishments of the past. Your destiny will not be determined by chance but by choice. By the smallest deed or choice, you might set in motion influences that could change your own destiny, and your future, that will affect your eternal destiny. Sometimes we feel that we have no destiny, or purpose, and we ask ourselves what God could ever do with me. But always remember that your finger is not as big as God's, your mind is not as big as his, your thoughts are not his. His dreams are bigger than yours.

God has given you a destiny; he has sketched out a plan for you. And there will be those that will question your destiny, but you remember God has called you, and anointed you, and chosen you. And it's time you fulfill your destiny. God will allow you to be inspired by the right person at the right time and he will allow people in your life to test you and persecute you so that you will find your destiny, and will do and will accomplish what God has chosen you to do for his kingdom.

Allow me to share this story with you. As a little child growing up in a Hindu home where my parents then used to practice Hinduism. It was never my interest to do what they were doing. A few times I was forced to practice Hinduism but never had the desire to do so but after receiving my healing at age seven from the Lord I had developed an interest in listening to preachers preaching on the radio, a program called "Christ is the Answer" I want to praise God for Christ is the Answer, anyway or I would admire great men and women of God ministering on television. So one day my father went and bought a fourteen inch black and white television set.

At that time that was all my dad could have afforded, so while my brothers and my sister would get excited about Texas Ranger, Night Riders and Fresh Prince of Bell Air, I would stay up very late in the night after they had gone to bed just to watch the late Dr. Oral Roberts tent revival. Watching this great man of God preach and lay hands on the sick my desire to preach the Gospel had increased tremendously so I decided to send a letter to Dr. Oral asking him to release his anointing on me and on several occasions, sending my few Guyana dollars I had then to plant faith seed. So my purpose of writing him is to be recognized by him and to let me know that I need his anointing. Well Dr. Roberts gone to be with the Lord and I've never gotten the opportunity to meet him personally or I've never received a reply from him saying if he got my letters or not. So as the years went by and I migrated to the USA my desires to preach the word had increased from desire to a passion to preach.

My passion has caused me to become very uncomfortable just like a woman who is pregnant and is about to give birth a to a fourteen pound baby. That is when I realized that it's not about man but what God has placed inside of you. Wanted my dreams to become reality I called upon every person I know to ordain me and give me a pastoral license because I wanted to preach the word. I was disappointed because no one felt that I was ready for the task. I was told to give up such a desire and passion because it's not an easy thing to request. But I know what I had inside of me and I personally refused to abort the desire and passion God has given me. As such, I seek the face of God and get on the Birthing floor and travail just like Mordecai did by gate of the kings palace and make my request known to God and sent my prayer request to every prayer partner I had known then. And Glory be to God in 2004 I started to give birth to that which was inside of me and started to fulfill my destiny.

I was able to give birth spiritually first to A prayer ministry called "As we answer the prophetic call to a Travailing Prayer" and then to the Emmanuel Full Gospel Assemblies of Churches and then the Robin Healing Ministries International "A Healing & Deliverance ministry that is now taking the Gospel of Jesus Christ to all the nations around the world demonstrating God's miraculous saving, healing and Deliverance power" and then the Emmanuel Bible Training Institute and then the Emmanuel Full Gospel Assemblies Ministerial Fellowship and the Bread of Life Ministry of Help.

I share all of that to say this, God has truly ordained and set you apart for something great, and you must recognize what he has placed in you. All God is saying to you today as you are reading this book, get into position, and if you are asking yourself what position you should get yourself in; well the answer is prayer, fasting, seeking his face and personal intercession and wait on the Lord to speak and when he speaks don't sit there and question what he is saying just do it. You must recognize what he is doing in your life and what are his plans for you. You have the power within yourself to recognize what God is doing and what he wants you to do. Don't wait for man to recognize it because if you can't recognize it then no one else will. You have been conceived with perfect health, wealth, ideas, blessings, wisdom, knowledge etc. You have something inside of you that Heaven is interested in. Song of Solomon 4:12 says a garden enclosed and barred is my sister, my [promised] bride—a spring shut up, a fountain sealed.

There is something inside of you that is so powerful that even the Abortionist-Satan can't even figure it out because God has placed it there and he is the only one who knows about it and wants you to recognize it just where you are because this is your season to give birth to that which he has promised you. God is waiting for you to discover what is inside of you so that he can journey you through the process to the birthing floor. You can only be going to the birthing floor if you are ready to make a sacrifice and give birth.

The birthing floor is ready to receive you and God has prepared a perfect and chosen vessel to help you through your birthing process but are you ready to give birth to that which God has placed inside of you. Probably you are saying well I don't think the time is right because there's a lot going on in life and I am getting real uncomfortable about all that is happening to me! Well the reason you are getting so uncomfortable is because your birthing season is now. And there is one way to discover your birthing season and that is when all hell has let loose on you, so forget about who is talking about you, just stand still and look what the Lord will do. Forget about how much education you have, forget about exposure. God will take care of every need, if he gave you a vision for a mission then he will make the provision just be obedient and position yourself for the birthing process. God has prepared someone to help you in the process just as how he positioned Mordecai to help Esther become queen.

Mordecai knew what Haman's plans were, if you read the book of Esther you will see that Mordecai told Esther all that Haman was doing and what his plans were, so Mordecai used Esther to approach the King for favor. And because of her obedience the Jewish nation was saved from being murdered and in the process Esther got favor and became the queen.

So God has designed a plan and prepared you for such a process but are you ready to come in compliance with God? You have to understand that the scripture says in Psalm 139:14 I will confess and praise You for You are fearful and wonderful and for the awful wonder of my birth! Wonderful are Your works, and that my inner self knows right well.

God wants you to know that you have been designed with a purpose to fulfill his will. And that which he has purposed in you is right inside of you, so that is why the Prophet Jeremiah says If I say, I will not make mention of [the Lord] or speak any more in His name, in my mind and heart it is as if there were a burning fire shut up in my bones. And I am weary of enduring and holding it in; I cannot [contain it any longer]. Jeremiah 20:9

God is currently calling forth people to give birth to that which he has conceived in them. Start making preparation for the Journey to the birthing floor. Put aside time to spend with God. The bible says seek ye first the kingdom of God and his righteousness then all these things shall be added unto you. You are about to birth something great in your life, this is the time to step out by faith and allow God to have his way in your life. God is calling forth the barren to conceive, according to Isaiah 54:1-20

SING, O barren one, you who did not bear; break forth into singing and cry aloud, you who did not travail with child! For the [spiritual] children of the desolate one will be more than the children of the married wife, says the Lord.

Enlarge the place of your tent, and let the curtains of your habitations be stretched out; spare not; lengthen your cords and strengthen your stakes,

For you will spread abroad to the right hand and to the left; and your offspring will possess the nations and make the desolate cities to be inhabited.

Fear not, for you shall not be ashamed; neither be confounded and depressed, for you shall not be put to shame. For you shall forget the shame of your youth, and you shall not [seriously] remember the reproach of your widowhood any more.

For your Maker is your Husband—the Lord of hosts is His name—and the Holy One of Israel is your Redeemer; the God of the whole earth He is called.

For the Lord has called you like a woman forsaken, grieved in spirit, and heart sore—even a wife [wooed and won] in youth, when she is [later] refused and scorned, says your God.

For a brief moment I forsook you, but with great compassion and mercy I will gather you [to Me] again.

In a little burst of wrath I hid My face from you for a moment, but with age-enduring love and kindness I will have compassion and mercy on you, says the Lord, your Redeemer.

For this is like the days of Noah to Me; as I swore that the waters of Noah should no more go over the earth, so have I sworn that I will not be angry with you or rebuke you.

For though the mountains should depart and the hills be shaken or removed, yet My love and kindness shall not depart from you, nor shall My covenant of peace and completeness be removed, says the Lord, Who has compassion on you.

O you afflicted [city], storm-tossed and not comforted, behold, I will set your stones in fair colors [in antimony to enhance their brilliance] and lay your foundations with sapphires.

And I will make your windows and pinnacles of [sparkling] agates or rubies, and your gates of [shining] carbuncles, and all your walls [of your enclosures] of precious stones.

And all your [spiritual] children shall be disciples [taught by the Lord and obedient to His will], and great shall be the peace and undisturbed composure of your children.

You shall establish yourself in righteousness (rightness, in conformity with God's will and order): you shall be far from even the thought of oppression or destruction, for you shall not fear, and from terror, for it shall not come near you.

Behold, they may gather together and stir up strife, but it is not from Me. Whoever stirs up strife against you shall fall and surrender to you.

Behold, I have created the smith who blows on the fire of coals and who produces a weapon for its purpose; and I have created the devastator to destroy.

But no weapon that is formed against you shall prosper, and every tongue that shall rise against you in judgment you shall show to be in the wrong. This [peace, righteousness, security, triumph over opposition] is the heritage of the servants of the Lord [those in whom the ideal Servant of the Lord is reproduced]; this is the righteousness or the vindication which they obtain from Me [this is that which I impart to them as their justification], says the Lord.

Don't let pass barrenness hold you back. Just PUSH pray until something happens at the birthing floor. You need to bring it out because no weapon that is formed against you shall prosper. Come on, stop worrying what others may say, get ready to start your journey to the birthing floor because this journey needs those that are willing to be an endurer. Psalm 104:31 says the glory of the LORD shall endure for ever: the LORD shall rejoice in his works.

CHAPTER THREE

THE BIRTHING OF PURPOSE & POSSIBILITIES

God will Make the Impossible to become Possible

Who has heard of such a thing? Who has seen such things? Shall a land be born in one day? Or shall a nation be brought forth in a moment? For as soon as Zion was in labor, she brought forth her children. Shall I bring to the [moment of] birth and not cause to bring forth? says the Lord. Shall I Who causes to bring forth shut the womb? Says your God. Isaiah 66:8-9

Have you ever asked the questions "Why am I here on earth?" or "Why God created me and for what purpose?" It is very important to check yourselves and inquire to know what your real purpose in life is. According to the word of God, I was created for his pleasure and not my own.

Revelation 4:11 says Worthy are You, our Lord and God, to receive the glory and the honor and dominion, for You created all things; by Your will they were [brought into being] and were created. What the Apostle John in Revelation was saying is that you were created by his pleasure, as such God expect you to be fruitful and multiply just as he declared in Genesis 1:28 "And God blessed them and said to them, Be fruitful, multiply, and fill the earth, and subdue it [using all its vast resources in the service of God and man]; and have dominion over the fish of the sea, the birds of the air, and over every living creature that moves upon the earth."

God never intend that any should be barren physically, spiritually, mentally, emotionally physiologically or financially and that is because he said he has placed in you a new Spirit. So get in your birth position now because he is about to cause contraction, so that you can give birth to your destiny. According to Ezekiel 11:19 "And I will give them one heart [a new heart] and I will put a new spirit within them; and I will take the stony [unnaturally hardened] heart out of their flesh, and will give them a heart of flesh [sensitive and responsive to the touch of their God]"

After examining what God spoke through the prophet Ezekiel, I have personally come to a place in my life to realize that God has more plans for us than we have known. Why did 2 Peter 3:9 says "The Lord does not delay and is not tardy or slow about what He promises, according to some people's conception of slowness, but He is long-suffering (extraordinarily patient) toward you, not desiring that any should perish, but that all should turn to repentance."

The reason why Peter said it clearly that God's plans and will is for none to perish, but that all should turn to repentance is because he needs vessel here on earth to use so that his plans can be accomplished.

There was a moment in time when God was watching over his people and was seeing the suffering they were going through, by the hands of Eli the compromising high priest and his degenerate sons. This has caused heaven contraction. God knew he had to do something to save his people.

The bible says God is touch by the very feelings of our infirmities. Hebrews 2:17 says "So it is evident that it was essential that He be made like His brethren in every respect, in order that He might become a merciful (sympathetic) and faithful High Priest in the things related to God, to make atonement and propitiation for the people's sins."

God knew it was time for a change and was looking for a prophet who he can speak to, a prophet who would be willing to hear from him and carrying out his instruction. As such, while earth was in need of a son, heaven was in need of a prophet. Heaven is in need of a vessel to place purpose, plans and vision and destiny in but the only place you can find this is at the birthing floor. So get yourself to the birthing floor that place of prayer and intercession so that you can know what heaven is about to release and at the same time position yourself to receive that which you are believing for.

Many times we missed God's revealed plans and blessing just because we are pitting ourselves based on the hardship of life but God knows what you are going through this very moment. He has what you want but are you willing to give him that which he needs. God needs us to break through walls of empty, formalistic, dry, staid, mediocre and meaningless professions of lip-service modes of prayer and intercession and break forth into a place of contrition and humility that will birth travailing prayer, a burden for the lost and hurting world, loving obedience to the Word, submission to one another, spontaneous and heartfelt praise and worship, along with supernatural signs, wonders and miracles.

God knows what you are going through in your life right now. If he knows the number of sand that is on the sea and the number of hair that is on your head, why don't you think that he knows what you are going through. Probably you are saying it is not that easy as how I may think but I do understand that. But are you ready to position yourself for your breakthrough, because the word of God says that all power is given unto you. Lets look at what Matthew 28:18 says "Jesus approached and, breaking the silence, said to them, All authority (all power of rule) in heaven and on earth has been given to Me."

God is saying to you that you have all power to overcome every situation in your life. Heaven is ready for you, but you need to ask yourself, Am I ready for heaven? Heaven is contracting but are you willing and ready to be used by God as a vessel to bring forth that which he has in store for you?

Just take a close look at Isaiah Chapter 54 and read it carefully and see Zion's joy over redemption, it has also a very personal, long-neglected, and often overlooked message for everyone of us, the lonely, the disappointed, the childless, the widow, the single parent, the heartbroken. It has all the glorious confidence and assurance, the incentive and understanding, for which broken hearts have longed throughout the ages!

Here God is saying to those of you who have broken dreams to praise in the very moment of brokenness and get yourself in position for favor. If you have a financial problems "SING" through your financial barrenness, God is saying to you with or without favor sing anyhow.

Oh how I love this Song: God on the Mountain – Words Quoted By Tracy G. Dartt

Life is easy when you're up on the mountain, And you've got peace of mind like you've never known. But then things change and you're down in the valley. Don't lose faith for you're never alone.

For the God on the mountain is still God in the valley. When things go wrong, He'll make it right. And the God of the good times is still God in the bad times. The God of the day is still God in the night.

You talk of faith when you're up on the mountain. Oh but the talk comes easy when life's at its best. But it's down in the valley of trials and temptation That's when faith is really put to the test.

For the God on the mountain is still God in the valley. When things go wrong, He'll make it right. And the God of the good times is still God in the bad times. The God of the day is still God in the night.

It is time to start looking at life beyond its ups and downs and begin to know he is the same God that saved you and brought you out of darkness into his marvelous light. So get yourself in birth position, heaven is contracting. God wants to hear from you even if you felt like you are barren. Sing in the midst of your situation, you are about to come forth if you sing. It is easy to sing when all is fine but it will not be easy to sing when you are barren in your finances, in your sickness, in your problems but "SING" position yourself and travail.

PUSH – Pray Until Something Happens

God wants to give you a paradigm shift but you have to make a choice if you are ready to change position and push forward. What God is saying in this very day and age is "Change Position" I am ready to do it for you. So stop laboring and PUSH get into birth position and allow God to work it for you. If you come to that place in your life and position yourself, God will hook you up. The choice is yours today to get into position, because the bible says that in the last days he will pour his Spirit on all flesh, Joel 2:28

Stop worrying about your tomorrow Matthew 6:25 says Therefore I tell you, stop being perpetually uneasy (anxious and worried) about your life, what you shall eat or what you shall drink; or about your body, what you shall put on. Is not life greater [in quality] than food, and the body [far above and more excellent] than clothing?

God is about to hook you up with the right job, the right business, the right person or the right people. God has a divine arrangement for you if you should only position yourself and allow him to work in you. Because according to his word he has called you. Take a look at Jeremiah Chapter One:

THE WORDS of Jeremiah son of Hilkiah, of the priests who were in Anathoth in the land of Benjamin [two or three miles north of Jerusalem],

To whom the word of the Lord came in the days of Josiah son of Amon king of Judah in the thirteenth year of his reign.

It came also in the days of Jehoiakim son of Josiah king of Judah until the end of the eleventh year of Zedekiah son of Josiah king of Judah, until the carrying away of Jerusalem into captivity in the fifth month

Then the word of the Lord came to me [Jeremiah], saying,

Before I formed you in the womb I knew [and] approved of you [as My chosen instrument], and before you were born I separated and set you apart, consecrating you; [and] I appointed you as a prophet to the nations.

Then said I, Ah, Lord God! Behold, I cannot speak, for I am only a youth.

But the Lord said to me, Say not, I am only a youth; for you shall go to all to whom I shall send you, and whatever I command you, you shall speak.

Be not afraid of them [their faces], for I am with you to deliver you, says the Lord.

Then the Lord put forth His hand and touched my mouth. And the Lord said to me, Behold, I have put My words in your mouth.

See, I have this day appointed you to the oversight of the nations and of the kingdoms to root out and pull down, to destroy and to overthrow, to build and to plant.

Moreover, the word of the Lord came to me, saying, Jeremiah, what do you see? And I said, I see a branch or shoot of an almond tree [the emblem of alertness and activity, blossoming in late winter].

Then said the Lord to me, You have seen well, for I am alert and active, watching over My word to perform it.

And the word of the Lord came to me the second time, saying, What do you see? And I said, I see a boiling pot, and the face of it is [tipped away] from the north [its mouth about to pour forth on the south, on Judea].

Then the Lord said to me, Out of the north the evil [which the prophets had foretold as the result of national sin] shall disclose itself and break forth upon all the inhabitants of the land.

For, behold, I will call all the tribes of the kingdoms of the north, says the Lord; and they will come and set every one his throne at the entrance of the gates of Jerusalem, against all its walls round about, and against all the cities of Judah [as God's judicial act, a consequence of Judah's wickedness].

And I will utter My judgments against them for all the wickedness of those who have forsaken Me, burned incense to other gods, and worshiped the works of their own hands [idols].

But you [Jeremiah], gird up your loins! Arise and tell them all that I command you. Do not be dismayed and break down at the sight of their faces, lest I confound you before them and permit you to be overcome.

For I, behold, I have made you this day a fortified city and an iron pillar and bronze walls against the whole land—against the [successive] kings of Judah, against its princes, against its priests, and against the people of the land [giving you divine strength which no hostile power can overcome].

And they shall fight against you, but they shall not [finally] prevail against you, for I am with you, says the Lord, to deliver you.

God is bringing you to a place where he can trade your sorrow for joy. Money is exchanged for goods but God wants you to exchange your pain for your breakthrough. Something good is about to come out of you, heaven is contracting and are ready to PUSH OUT that which is you. If you have the question well what good can come out of me? Well they ask the same question, what good can come out of Nazareth-Well the good news is JESUS did.

So stand still and see God working on your behalf, just watch and pray, get to the birthing floor and get yourself in birth position, your birth position is a new dimension. Stop listening to what the enemy has to say to you. All the devil is saying is that you can't make it, you can't get to that dimension. Well just to let you know he is a liar and the father of it too, what is your brand? Who told you that you cannot make it-who told you that you would not mount up to anything?

I was personally told that I would not mount up to anything, that I can never live up to my dreams. I was told that my ministry will not make it more than six months, but glory be to God, the Father, Jesus the Son and the Holy Spirit who is my comforter. I now prove the devil wrong because God is taking me to places that I have never dreamed or imagined I would go or could have gone. Its time that you make demands on heaven for your life. Hannah did, she pursued after God's heart and made demands on heaven without man's permission and succeeded.

Take a close look at the life of Hannah and how she positioned herself and made demands on heaven and at the same time see what God has done for her. In the midst of barrenness Hannah went down to the Altar of the Tabernacle, a place she made her birthing floor and cried out to the Lord. Peninnah tried to impress upon Hannah that she will never have children, tried to tell her she will remain barren but Hannah knew how to travail, so she journeyed to

Birthing Floor

the birthing floor and positioned herself for conception and all this happened through prayer and personal intercession.

The biggest question here before you continue to read this book. Are you ready to take a journey to the birthing floor and position yourself for your conception? Are you ready to birth your dreams and visions and let it become a reality. Heaven is ready for you; God's promises must be fulfilled in your life. Why crying day by day worrying about what people are saying about you, it's time for you to position yourself for a change. Shake off every criticism and discouraging words off your life and break yourself into a new dimension with your physical and spiritual life.

Take a look at the book of 1 Samuel 1:1-28 here the bible says "There was a certain man of Ramathaim-zophim, of the hill country of Ephraim, named Elkanah son of Jeroham, the son of Elihu, the son of Tohu, the son of Zuph, an Ephraimite.

He had two wives, one named Hannah and the other named Peninnah. Peninnah had children, but Hannah had none.

This man went from his city year by year to worship and sacrifice to the Lord of hosts at Shiloh, where Hophni and Phinehas, the two sons of Eli, were the Lord's priests.

When the day came that Elkanah sacrificed, he would give to Peninnah his wife and all her sons and daughters portions [of the sacrificial meat].

But to Hannah he gave a double portion, for he loved Hannah, but the Lord had given her no children.

[This embarrassed and grieved Hannah] and her rival provoked her greatly to vex her, because the Lord had left her childless.

So it was year after year; whenever Hannah went up to the Lord's house, Peninnah provoked her, so she wept and did not eat.

Then Elkanah her husband said to her, Hannah, why do you cry? And why do you not eat? And why are you grieving? Am I not more to you than ten sons?

So Hannah rose after they had eaten and drunk in Shiloh. Now Eli the priest was sitting on his seat beside a post of the temple (tent) of the Lord.

And [Hannah] was in distress of soul, praying to the Lord and weeping bitterly.

She vowed, saying, O Lord of hosts, if You will indeed look on the affliction of Your handmaid and [earnestly] remember, and not forget Your handmaid but will give me a son, I will give him to the Lord all his life; no razor shall touch his head.

And as she continued praying before the Lord, Eli noticed her mouth. Hannah was speaking in her heart; only her lips moved but her voice was not heard. So Eli thought she was drunk.

Eli said to her, how long will you be intoxicated? Put wine away from you. But Hannah answered, No, my lord, I am a woman of a sorrowful spirit. I have drunk neither wine nor strong drink, but I was pouring out my soul before the Lord.

Regard not your handmaid as a wicked woman; for out of my great complaint and bitter provocation I have been speaking.

Then Eli said, Go in peace, and may the God of Israel grant your petition which you have asked of Him.

Hannah said, Let your handmaid find grace in your sight. So [she] went her way and ate, her countenance no longer sad.

The family rose early the next morning, worshiped before the Lord, and returned to their home in Ramah. Elkanah knew Hannah his wife, and the Lord remembered her.

Hannah became pregnant and in due time bore a son and named him Samuel [heard of God], Because, she said, I have asked him of the Lord.

And Elkanah and all his house went up to offer to the Lord the yearly sacrifice and pay his vow.

But Hannah did not go, for she said to her husband, I will not go until the child is weaned, and then I will bring him, that he may appear before the Lord and remain there as long as he lives.

Elkanah her husband said to her, Do what seems best to you. Wait until you have weaned him; only may the Lord establish His word. So Hannah remained and nursed her son until she weaned him.

When she had weaned him, she took him with her, with a three-year-old bull, an ephah of flour, and a skin bottle of wine [to pour over the burnt offering for a sweet odor], and brought Samuel to the Lord's house in Shiloh. The child was growing.

Then they slew the bull, and brought the child to Eli. Hannah said, Oh, my lord! As your soul lives, my lord, I am the woman who stood by you here praying to the Lord.

For this child I prayed, and the Lord has granted my petition made to Him. Therefore I have given him to the Lord; as long as he lives he is given to the Lord. And they worshiped the Lord there.

Hannah positioned herself for a victory and breakthrough. Her story is a story of victory - it's a story of reposition - it's a story of new life - it's a story of deliverance - it's a story about a changed life - it's about intercession, it's about obedience, it's about the privilege of being used by God in his plans and purposes. It's about how God intervened in an ordinary woman's life just because she knew how to position herself.

God did something new in Hannah - something remarkable. She was a remarkable woman but she wasn't always remarkable because people used to think of her as a barren women with fruitfulness in her life, so my question to you today what do people think about you right now, how do you see yourself and how do people see you? Hannah was depressed, despondent, and downcast because of all that she was going through in her life. Probably this is you in a different situation; maybe you are barren in your finances or spiritual life. But God intervened in Hannah's life - he did something new in her and she was never the same again. So if you allow God he can do the same for you today, nothing is impossible with him.

Today your life's story can be a story of victory and a story of breakthrough. But you have to make a serious decision in your life and that is to position yourself on the birthing floor and allow God to work in your heart and lift your faith.

Hannah was an ordinary woman had a normal life like most people but she had a problem. Her problem was bareness and in those days to be barren was considered a kind of disgrace; it was a reason to feel ashamed. Many believed that there was something wrong that God had closed here womb.

I remembered very clearly when one woman walked up to me in one of my miracle crusades and with tears in her eyes she said I can't have children and my marriage is in distraught because of my barrenness. As such her in-laws would talk about her and ridicule her claiming she has a curse on her life. According to the Word of God Hannah was in a position where she was laughed at and talked about also but she decided to do something about her situation. I want to let you know that no one has the power to do something about your situation but you. You have the power to stop the devil from working in your life, only you can bring yourself to that place of deliverance or breakthrough, just as Hannah did.

Probably you are saying well all seems to be well with BUT? There has been a big but in your life, well although Hannah was laughed at and had no children, Elkanah her husband loved her more than Peninnah. It wasn't enough for Hannah - Elkanah even gave her a double portion of meat, to show her how much he loved her and because she had no children. But it wasn't enough. Hannah was miserable.

On top of all that, because Peninnah was so jealous that Elkanah loved Hannah more than her, she provoked Hannah, and taunted her, so that Hannah would weep and would not eat. It's likely that the problems in their relationship were heightened at this time of annual sacrifice, perhaps because they were together more than usual or because it was when Elkanah showed his affection more to Hannah

It was the more disappointing because they were there to worship God -Shiloh was the place God had commanded his people to worship - they were forbidden to worship elsewhere. It was not the time or place for quarrelling or rivalry. This is what you should know and that is to tell you that the Devil knows that you are God's favorite that is why he is trying to put pressure on you. But watch out, as you enter into the birthing floor and position yourself and travail and call upon the name of the Lord, your blessing will be greater than the former.

This difficulty between Hannah and Peninnah went on year after year. I wonder how many years it was - maybe five, maybe fifteen - long enough for Hannah to become depressed - her face was downcast - she was weeping - it affected her relationship with her husband "Elkanah her husband would say to her, 'Hannah, why are you weeping? Why don't you eat? Why are you downhearted? Don't I mean more to you than ten sons?

This brings me to a point to ask how long have you been in despair - how long have you been depressed? How long has that difficult situation been going on? This isn't just about overcoming depression or despair. It's about being desperate – you can be desperate about many things - maybe you've been yearning for the Lord to do something new in you, yearning for something more in your Christian life - maybe you feel stale, stuck in a rut, you want to feel the excitement you once knew. Then position yourself now. Don't you wait for another prophesy, don't wait for someone to pray for you, don't wait for a minute more to pass but change your desperation from trouble to desperation for change and breakthrough now.

Maybe it's been going on for years - you're fed up going through the motions. Maybe you're longing for him to show you visions, to prophesy, to move in words of knowledge. Maybe you want him to give you a new ministry, to shake you up, to do something dynamic in your life. Maybe you've got such a desire in you to get closer to him, to be more intimate with him, to go deeper in worship. Maybe you don't know what you want - maybe you're simply hungry and thirsty. I wonder, how long the cry of your heart has been, "How much longer Lord?"

Let that change come to you now, I declare and decree it over your life right now as you are reading this book. Don't you ever wait for another minute to pass you by. Stop reading right now, throw your hands up in the air where ever you are and shout Jesus help, help me now Lord and receive your change now in Jesus' name. OK you can read on now. Glory be to God the father, Jesus the son and the Holy Spirit. Amen

I can image that Hannah could not bear it any more and decided to take action, so she stood up. It is time for you to take action now. I remembered when we purchased our first church building; there were so many problems to get the paper work done to move in to have fellowship. And because there was a huge delay in getting all the paper work ready the seller wanted to cancel the deal, I knew what was the promises of God, and after going through so much ordeal with the seller I called upon the elders of the ministry and said we are going to stand up and take this battle in spiritual warfare and prayer. I clearly remembered that I could not take it personally anymore, I became very desperate. As such, I called a day of fasting and prayer and decided to take a stand and the elders and I went before God to intervene in the situation with the building.

In the midst of the prayer meeting at the midnight hour God spoke a word to me. God said read Exodus 14:13-16 and I began to read and this is what the word of God spoke to me:

Moses told the people, Fear not; stand still (firm, confident, undismayed) and see the salvation of the Lord which He will work for you today. For the Egyptians you have seen today you shall never see again.

The Lord will fight for you, and you shall hold your peace and remain at rest.

The Lord said to Moses, Why do you cry to Me? Tell the people of Israel to go forward!

Lift up your rod and stretch out your hand over the sea and divide it, and the Israelites shall go on dry ground through the midst of the sea.

Within two weeks after I stood up and sought the face of God and he gave me that word, every paper work started to come forth and the process sped up and within one month from that day we moved into our ministry headquarter.

According to the word of God "Hannah stood up". Three little words, but they say such a lot. It says that eventually Hannah couldn't take any more - she made a decision to do something about her situation and that is she positioned herself. She said, enough is enough, this was a breakthrough for Hannah — she stood up - she rose up above her circumstances - she took a step. Only she could have done it. Maybe you need to experience a breakthrough today — But only you can do it. Hannah decided that she would rise up and head to the birthing floor which was the altar of the tabernacle only just to position herself for change.

Instead of staying in her despair, in her circumstances, she stood up and decided to pray to the Lord and with that came release from all the pent-up bitterness. With many tears she poured her heart out, according to verse fifteen "I was pouring out my soul to the Lord."

Hannah's prayer was true pleading to the Lord, with many tears, out of a desperate heart. The Holy Spirit hadn't been given in those days - we read about a few occasions when the Holy Spirit came upon people at particular times - but because of Jesus each one of us can personally know the Holy Spirit and his power in our lives.

Romans 8:26 says, "In the same way, the Spirit helps us in our weakness. We do not know what we ought to pray for, but the Spirit himself intercedes for us with groans that words cannot express. And he who searches our hearts knows the mind of the spirit, because the Spirit intercedes for the saints in accordance with God's will." Groans, tears, anguish, sorrow - the Holy Spirit helps us - intercedes for us at those times when we have no words.

Hannah poured out her heart to God - she said she was deeply troubled, in great anguish and grief. So distraught was she that Eli thought she was drunk and rebuked her. We need to feel things deeply as we pray and travail at the birthing floor - we need to weep sometimes, for ourselves and on behalf of others - it touches God's heart as he sees the depth of our desire, our burden. Eli misunderstood her - it's likely that there were drunken women at the door of the tabernacle, In chapter two it says that Eli's sons slept with some of them.

But Eli was at fault here because he accused Hannah unjustly. If he'd taken a bit more time in his observation of her he may have realized that someone who is drunk is more likely to be loud and causing a scene than to be silent and composed as Hannah was. Sometimes we feel misunderstood and that we're being accused wrongly.

We would do well to follow Hannah's example here - she didn't react badly and counter-accuse Eli because of his sons' behavior - no she respectfully and quietly explained herself. She needed to be understood - she explained her anguish to Eli and he spoke peace to her. We need to press through in prayer until we reach a place of peace. We also sometimes need to explain to others if we feel misunderstood.

Hannah spoke up - she was quite bold - Eli was a priest who spent his whole life ministering before the Lord. It would have been quite unusual for a woman to correct a man, particularly a man of his status - she addressed him "my Lord". Realizing he'd judged her wrongly, he then said to her, "Go in peace, and may the God of Israel grant you what you have asked of him." Hannah then went on her way and ate something and her face was no longer downcast.

That's interesting - having spent time in prayer and unburdening herself to the Lord, receiving peace and a blessing from Eli, she felt much better and was then able to eat. She looked different - her face was no longer downcast. Have you ever witnessed that kind of dramatic change in someone? Ever had the privilege of praying for people over the years and seeing the change in a person's face when God has done something special - when peace has come to a troubled soul full of anxiety or despair. People look lighter, the whole countenance changes, the eyes sparkle - it's wonderful. Praise the Lord!

Today can be your day just like Hannah, but you first have to decide to rise up from your situation and go before God. Hannah stood up the bible says and she catapulted herself and positioned herself for a paradigm shift. Make your prayer closet your birthing floor and position yourself for a change. Change in your finances, change in your spiritual walk with God, change in your prayer life, change in your ministry, change how you feel about others. You are in for a paradigm shift in your life, in your finances, in your walk with God, further more in every area of your life.

Hannah came to the end of herself and realized that only God could give her, her heart's desire. She made a vow that if God gave her a son then she would give him to the Lord for the rest of his life. This was not a vow taken lightly - it would cost her dearly - let's be serious when we make a vow or promise to the Lord, to see it through.

God granted Hannah a son. She named him Samuel, saying, "Because I asked the Lord for him". Samuel sounds like the Hebrew for "heard of God". In her prayer in chapter 2 Hannah says, "for the Lord is a God who knows".

Hannah was quick to praise and glorify God for this answer to her prayer. In verse one of chapter two she says "My heart rejoices in the Lord" - it reminded me of Mary's prayer after she'd been told that she would give birth to the Saviour, Jesus. She said "My soul glorifies the Lord and my spirit rejoices in God my Saviour". Let's be quick to praise and glorify God for all that he does in our lives.

Hannah kept her son until he was weaned, probably about three years old - it was usual for women to breastfeed their children until they were three in those days, when it was felt they could be entrusted to others. I believed she held on to him as long as she could and didn't go to the yearly sacrifice at Shiloh because she knew once she took her son there, she could not bring him back.

Elkanah bore with her knowing how hard it would be to let Samuel go, but said, "only may the Lord make good his word." After he was weaned she took him with her to Shiloh because she'd made a vow before God. She had to let him go. She took Samuel to Eli - how hard it must have been for her to leave him, such a small child, but she'd made a vow and had to be obedient. There is a cost to obedience. The result of Hannah's obedience - her heart rejoiced, she praised God even though she'd left Samuel, not knowing at that time whether she would have any more children.

Every year Hannah would go to the annual sacrifice at Shiloh and take Samuel a little robe. Eli blessed Elkanah and Hannah and prayed she would have more children, "the Lord was gracious to Hannah; she conceived and gave birth to three sons and two daughters."

What happened to Samuel? He stayed and ministered before the Lord under Eli - God called him and he became a prophet to all Israel.

God's purposes were worked out through Hannah. She could have continued in despair as she had for many years. But she stood up - she rose above her circumstances and made a decision to seek the Lord - to pour it all out to him - to ask him for the impossible. How long had she been childless? How long have you been in your circumstances that caused you despair?

You need to seek the lord, surrender to him, allow your desperation to show. Eli thought Hannah was drunk. Pour it out to him. Receive his peace. Trust him for the solution. "Her face was no longer downcast".

If you've received something from the Lord, it shows in your face - you look different - people will remark on it. You've changed because you've been in his presence and he has given you your heart's desire.

Are you willing to stand up like Hannah did and pour out your heart to him and ask him for what you need? Do you need a breakthrough? Do you need deliverance? Do you want God to intervene in your life? How desperate are you? Who knows what he can do with your life? He does - because he, "the Lord is a God who knows".

Contraction Zone – God is working on me, heaven is contracting:

There is a breakthrough that is waiting for you, did you ever take a close up look at Deuteronomy Chapter 28:1-13 if you will listen diligently to the voice of the Lord your God, being watchful to do all His commandments which I command you this day, the Lord your God will set you high above all the nations of the earth.

And all these blessings shall come upon you and overtake you if you heed the voice of the Lord your God. Blessed shall you be in the city and blessed shall you be in the field.

Blessed shall be the fruit of your body and the fruit of your ground and the fruit of your beasts, the increase of your cattle and the young of your flock.

Blessed shall be your basket and your kneading trough. Blessed shall you be when you come in and blessed shall you be when you go out.

The Lord shall cause your enemies who rise up against you to be defeated before your face; they shall come out against you one way and flee before you seven ways.

The Lord shall command the blessing upon you in your storehouse and in all that you undertake. And He will bless you in the land which the Lord your God gives you.

The Lord will establish you as a people holy to Himself, as He has sworn to you, if you keep the commandments of the Lord your God and walk in His ways.

And all people of the earth shall see that you are called by the name [and in the presence of] the Lord, and they shall be afraid of you.

And the Lord shall make you have a surplus of prosperity, through the fruit of your body, of your livestock, and of your ground, in the land which the Lord swore to your fathers to give you.

The Lord shall open to you His good treasury, the heavens, to give the rain of your land in its season and to bless all the work of your hands; and you shall lend to many nations, but you shall not borrow.

And the Lord shall make you the head, and not the tail; and you shall be above only, and you shall not be beneath, if you heed the commandments of the Lord your God which I command you this day and are watchful to do them.

And you shall not turn aside from any of the words which I command you this day, to the right hand or to the left, to go after other gods to serve them.

You have the power to declare and decree over your life right now that God will bring you into a position of blessings. You have got the power to shut anything that is not of God in your life right now. SHUT IT DOWN – you are about to be guided through your prophetic delivery because you are about to give birth to something new in the realm of spirit.

Heaven is inducing labors – God wants to bring your breakthrough and that which you're been asking for faster than you may think. God does not want you to labor and get worried and being in defect too long. Too long the devil has been wearing you out with situation and circumstances, but God is inducing labor to get this done fast.

In spite of your circumstance, God is getting ready to rearrange you even before you finish reading this book, because you got the capacity and so get ready to stretch yourself as you wait on the Lord. Every problem you are facing in life right now is just to stretch you for a bigger blessing.

Are you ready to give birth to your destiny, so confess it to God, you must understand that whatever comes out of your mouth will determine your destiny The greatest problem in yourself is not the devil it is your ignorance. Lose yourself and break out of ignorance. Know who you are – you are God's name brand. You must declare and decree it that you are God's chosen one.

CHAPTER FOUR

THE BIRTHING OF SPIRUTAL JOURNEY TO WITH MEET WITH GOD

There I will meet with you and, from above the mercy seat, from between the two cherubim that are upon the ark of the Testimony, I will speak intimately with you of all which I will give you in commandment to the Israelites. Exodus 25:22 (Amplified Bible)

I want to start this chapter of the Birthing Floor by asking you this question. Are you prepared to journey yourself to the Birthing Floor, a place where God wants you? I want to take you to a journey in the realm of the Spirit to a place where God's will, plans and purpose will be fulfilled in your life.

First you must have in mind before you take this spiritual journey that only God can take you there. Just as Michael Gungor wrote it his song Wrap me in your arms.

"There is a God who loves me, who wraps me in His arms, and that is the place where I'm changed, and that's where I belong. Take me to that place Lord, to that secret place where I can be with you. You can make me like you, wrap me in your arms"

To give birth to that treasure or idea that is in you, you first have to go through the process of sanctification and journey yourself to the birthing floor. God wants to wrap you in his arms and take you to that place, which is the birthing floor a place of sanctification for a change of service to him, a place of consecration – a change of standing before him, The Place of Regeneration – A change of nature for him, the Place of Conversion – A change of life for him.

God is going to bless those who have the faith of expectance, and those who know that they are blessed. As I look at a biblical role model Esther and how she journeyed herself into the palace. Esther did not get her position in the palace by just daydreaming. She journeyed with endurance, obedience to Mordecai and the passion within herself for the position and so she pursued with every being that she had for such a blessing.

Are you ready to do what Esther did and are you prepared to travail and take chances just the way Esther did? Let's take a look at the book of Esther and see how she journeyed herself to the palace position with the help of her uncle Mordecai and you begin to pattern yourselves for your journey and prepare yourselves for favors.

First of all you must come to a place in your life where you can recognize that God needs you to make intercession on behalf of yourself and even for the lost and dying world. God needs someone who can cry out to him on behalf of the lost and hurting world. Esther is a perfect example of this; she was inspired by her uncle Mordecai, and fulfilled this role of intercession and in the midst of her intercession he give birth to her destiny, she became the queen of the palace.

I want you to take a close look at the book of Esther chapter three, four and five. Because I want to assure you that God will speak something in your life. Probably you read these three chapters before, but I want to guarantee you that you will have a fresh revelation from God this time as you read it.

Esther Journeyed to the Birthing Floor "The Palace"

Let's take a look at the book of Esther Chapter Three, four and five and see the process Esther took as she journeyed herself to the Palace.

AFTER THESE things, King Ahasuerus promoted Haman the son of Hammedatha the Agagite and advanced him and set his seat above all the princes who were with him.

And all the king's servants who were at the king's gate bowed down and did reverence to Haman, for the king had so commanded concerning him. But Mordecai did not bow down or do him reverence.

Then the king's servants who were at the king's gate said to Mordecai, Why do you transgress the king's command?

Now when they spoke to him day after day and he paid no attention to them, they told Haman to see whether Mordecai's conduct would stand, for he had told them that he was a Jew.

And when Haman saw that Mordecai did not bow down or do him reverence, he was very angry.

But he scorned laying hands only on Mordecai. So since they had told him Mordecai's nationality, Haman sought to destroy all the Jews, the people of Mordecai, throughout the whole kingdom of Ahasuerus.

In the first month, the month of Nisan, in the twelfth year of King Ahasuerus, Haman caused Pur, that is, lots, to be cast before him day after day [to find a lucky day for his venture], month after month, until the twelfth, the month of Adar.

Then Haman said to King Ahasuerus, There is a certain people scattered abroad and dispersed among the peoples in all the provinces of your kingdom; their laws are different from every other people, neither do they keep the king's laws. Therefore it is not for the king's profit to tolerate them.

If it pleases the king, let it be decreed that they be destroyed, and I will pay 10,000 talents of silver into the hands of those who have charge of the king's business, that it may be brought into the king's treasuries.

And the king took his signet ring from his hand [with which to seal his letters by the king's authority] and gave it to Haman son of Hammedatha the Agagite, the Jews' enemy.

And the king said to Haman, The silver is given to you, the people also, to do with them as it seems good to you.

Then the king's secretaries were called in on the thirteenth day of the first month, and all that Haman had commanded was written to the king's chief rulers and to the governors who were over all the provinces and to the princes of each people, to every province in its own script and to each people in their own language; it was written in the name of King Ahasuerus and it was sealed with the king's [signet] ring.

And letters were sent by special messengers to all the king's provinces—to destroy, to slay, and to do away with all Jews, both young and old, little children and women, in one day, the thirteenth day of the twelfth month, the month of Adar, and to seize their belongings as spoil.

A copy of the writing was to be published and given out as a decree in every province to all the people to be ready for that day.

The special messengers went out in haste by order of the king, and the decree was given out in Shushan, the capital. And the King and Haman sat down to drink, but the city of Shushan was perplexed [at the strange and alarming decree].

God positioned Mordecai to help Esther through this journey to the palace

Esther Chapter Four

NOW WHEN Mordecai learned all that was done, [he] rent his clothes and put on sackcloth with ashes and went out into the midst of the city and cried with a loud and bitter cry.

He came and stood before the king's gate, for no one might enter the king's gate clothed with sackcloth.

And in every province, wherever the king's commandment and his decree came, there was great mourning among the Jews, with fasting, weeping, and wailing, and many lay in sackcloth and ashes.

When Esther's maids and her attendants came and told it to her, the queen was exceedingly grieved and distressed. She sent garments to clothe Mordecai, with orders to take his sackcloth from off him, but he would not receive them.

Then Esther called for Hathach, one of the king's attendants whom he had appointed to attend her, and ordered him to go to Mordecai to learn what this was and why it was.

So Hathach went out to Mordecai in the open square of the city, which was in front of the king's gate.

And Mordecai told him of all that had happened to him, and the exact sum of money that Haman had promised to pay to the king's treasuries for the Jews to be destroyed.

[Mordecai] also gave him a copy of the decree to destroy them, that was given out in Shushan, that he might show it to Esther, explain it to her, and charge her to go to the king, make supplication to him, and plead with him for the lives of her people.

And Hathach came and told Esther the words of Mordecai.

Then Esther spoke to Hathach and gave him a message for Mordecai, saying,

All the king's servants and the people of the king's provinces know that any person, be it man or woman, who shall go into the inner court to the king without being called shall be put to death; there is but one law for him, except [him] to whom the king shall hold out the golden scepter, that he may live. But I have not been called to come to the king for these thirty days.

And they told Mordecai what Esther said.

Then Mordecai told them to return this answer to Esther, Do not flatter yourself that you shall escape in the king's palace any more than all the other Jews.

For if you keep silent at this time, relief and deliverance shall arise for the Jews from elsewhere, but you and your father's house will perish. And who knows but that you have come to the kingdom for such a time as this and for this very occasion?

Then Esther told them to give this answer to Mordecai,

Go, gather together all the Jews that are present in Shushan, and fast for me; and neither eat nor drink for three days, night or day. I also and my maids will fast as you do. Then I will go to the king, though it is against the law; and if I perish, I perish.

So Mordecai went away and did all that Esther had commanded him.

Esther journeyed through in spite of feelings and take risk as she entered her final destination into the palace

Esther Chapter Five

ON THE third day [of the fast] Esther put on her royal robes and stood in the royal or inner court of the king's palace opposite his [throne room]. The king was sitting on his throne, facing the main entrance of the palace.

And when the king saw Esther the queen standing in the court, she obtained favor in his sight, and he held out to [her] the golden scepter that was in his hand. So Esther drew near and touched the tip of the scepter.

Then the king said to her what will you have Queen Esther? What is your request? It shall be given you, even to the half of the kingdom.

And Esther said, If it seems good to the king, let the king and Haman come this day to the dinner that I have prepared for the king.

Then the king said, Cause Haman to come quickly, that what Esther has said may be done. So the king and Haman came to the dinner that Esther had prepared.

And during the serving of wine, the king said to Esther, What is your petition? It shall be granted you. And what is your request? Even to the half of the kingdom, it shall be performed.

Then Esther said, My petition and my request is: If I have found favor in the sight of the king and if it pleases the king to grant my petition and to perform my request, let the king and Haman come tomorrow to the dinner that I shall prepare for them; and I will do tomorrow as the king has said.

Haman went away that day joyful and elated in heart. But when he saw Mordecai at the king's gate refusing to stand up or show fear before him, he was filled with wrath against Mordecai.

Nevertheless, Haman restrained himself and went home. There he sent and called for his friends and Zeresh his wife.

And Haman recounted to them the glory of his riches, the abundance of his [ten] sons, all the things in which the king had promoted him, and how he had advanced him above the princes and servants of the king.

Haman added, Yes, and today Queen Esther did not let any man come with the king to the dinner she had prepared but myself; and tomorrow also I am invited by her together with the king.

Yet all this benefits me nothing as long as I see Mordecai the Jew sitting at the king's gate.

Then Zeresh his wife and all his friends said to him, Let a gallows be made, fifty cubits [seventy-five feet] high, and in the morning speak to the king, that Mordecai may be hanged on it; then you go in merrily with the king to the dinner. And the thing pleased Haman, and he caused the gallows to be made.

First of all the book of Esther started by revealing the unusual journey that Esther took to become queen of a Gentile nation. In chapter three of the book of Esther you can see that Haman was promoted and his promotion has caused Esther to journey to king Ahasuerus for favor.

Probably you are saying to yourself every one is getting their breakthrough and blessing but it seems like God has forgotten me. Well I want to let you know stop worrying about someone else's breakthrough and start journeying yourself to the birthing floor. The birthing floor is a place of prayer and intercession waiting on God as you keep travailing for favor.

Isaiah the prophet says they that wait upon the Lord shall renew their strength. So while everyone else seems to be having their breakthrough and it seems like yours are not coming, then I say wait upon the Lord.

Yes Haman the Agagite has a promotion, he became the Prime Minister to Ahasuerus and just remember this one of the perks that came with his new position was the homage people were required to pay to Him. And that was the king commanded everyone to bow before and give reverence to him and he deeply enjoyed that but that was just a cause to stir something into Mordecai's life to help Esther to begin her journey to the birthing floor which is the King's chamber.

Stop worrying about who got promotion before you or who is using their promotion to manipulate you with their power. God is about to turn things around on your behalf. God will cause the right person to come in your life to help position you and to help you start your journey to birthing floor where you will be able to give birth to every promise which has been held up for so long.

There is a reason why you are going through so many situations, problems and persecutions. That is to help prepare you and help position you for the greater things that God has in store for you. The word of God says in the book of Exodus 14:13-16 as I mentioned in chapter one that God will fight for you and put people in your path to stand with you. God used Mordecai to help Esther through the process to birthing floor. God uses a situation between Mordecai and Haman to bring Esther to the palace. Problem arose when Mordecai refused to bow before Haman.

The king's servants, who suspected how this would be received by Haman, tried to convince Mordecai to bow, but he steadfastly refused. There will be time in your life when you need to refuse things that are not of God, so that he can bless you in due season. Now you must understand who Mordecai was, he was a Jew and would bow only to God! There are times when the only course for pragmatism is to kneel before principle. When a person refuses to violate his principles—that is, he does the right thing, he will suffer the consequences of his action. The servants, curious to see whether this impudence would be tolerated, informed Haman of Mordecai's refusal.

Haman became enraged. He took it as a personal affront and determined to execute Mordecai. The servants had also informed him that Mordecai was a Jew. Haman, overcome with rage and wounded pride, decided to kill not only Mordecai, but also all of his people, the Jews in Persia. Haman approached King Ahasuerus with his plan. It is time that you take your stand and do what God says for you to do and that is Be Still and Know that I am God.

The king so approved of Haman's plan that he excused Haman from paying the ten thousand talents of silver to the treasury. The king gave Haman his signet ring and summoned the scribes on the thirteenth day of the first month to write a decree to be distributed throughout the empire. All the Jews were to be killed on the thirteenth day of the twelfth month. A decree sealed with the king's ring could not be revoked. Haman's action cast a long shadow over the Jewish people. Those were dark days for the Jews.

Always remember that Satan the Arborist and you cannot mix well together. If you ever did, it is to the detriment of the body of Christ. As long as the body of Christ maintains its identity, it will resist any overtures from Satan.

The hostility between you and Satan is more than passive dislike for each other. The devil has been relentless in his quest to destroy you who are carrying the promises of God. He is not resting because he knows his time is drawing close. As we approach the return of Christ, Satan has stepped up his attack on every believer. He leaves no stone unturned, no plan untried, and no saint untouched in his plans against you. He slips falsehood into truth until it becomes difficult to discern between the two. He tries to intimidate you by unleashing persecution in your direction. He pushes the pursuit of prosperity to the world, hoping to lull them to sleep.

Satan is doing everything in his power to extinguish the fire of God that is in you. He has made this a dark day in which to live. He wants to abort and steal that which God has placed inside of you but he just can't. And even the things that we have lost in the process while we were yet sinners God has promised to restore it to us. God said in the Isaiah 45:

THUS SAYS the Lord to His anointed, to Cyrus, whose right hand I have held to subdue nations before him, and I will unarm and ungird the loins of kings to open doors before him, so that gates will not be shut.

I will go before you and level the mountains [to make the crooked places straight]; I will break in pieces the doors of bronze and cut asunder the bars of iron.

And I will give you the treasures of darkness and hidden riches of secret places, that you may know that it is I, the Lord, the God of Israel, Who calls you by your name.

For the sake of Jacob My servant, and of Israel My chosen, I have called you by your name. I have surnamed you, though you have not known Me.

I am the Lord, and there is no one else; there is no God besides Me. I will gird and arm you, though you have not known Me,

That men may know from the east and the rising of the sun and from the west and the setting of the sun that there is no God besides Me. I am the Lord, and no one else [is He].

I form the light and create darkness, I make peace [national well-being] and I create [physical] evil (calamity); I am the Lord, Who does all these things.

Let fall in showers, you heavens, from above, and let the skies rain down righteousness [the pure, spiritual, heaven-born possibilities that have their foundation in the holy being of God]; let the earth open, and let them [skies and earth] sprout forth salvation, and let righteousness germinate and spring up [as plants do] together; I the Lord have created it.

Woe to him who strives with his Maker!—a worthless piece of broken pottery among other pieces equally worthless [and yet presuming to strive with his Maker]! Shall the clay say to him who fashions it, What do you think you are making? or, Your work has no handles?

Woe to him [who complains against his parents that they have begotten him] who says to a father, What are you begetting? or to a woman, With what are you in travail?

11Thus says the Lord, the Holy One of Israel, and its Maker: Would you question Me about things to come concerning My children, and concerning the work of My hands [would you] command Me?

12I made the earth and created man upon it. I, with My hands, stretched out the heavens, and I commanded all their host.

13I will raise [Cyrus] up in righteousness [willing in every way that which is right and proper], and I will direct all his ways; he will build My city, and he will let My captives go, not for hire or for a bribe, says the Lord of hosts.

14Thus says the Lord: The labor and wealth of Egypt and the merchandise of Ethiopia and the Sabeans, men of stature, shall come over to you and they shall be yours; they shall follow you; in chains [of subjection to you] they shall come over, and they shall fall down before you; they shall make supplication to you, saying, Surely God is with you, and there is no other, no God besides Him.

¹⁵Truly You are a God Who hides Himself, O God of Israel, the Savior.

¹⁶They shall be put to shame, yes, confounded, all of them; they who are makers of idols shall go off into confusion together.

¹⁷But Israel shall be saved by the Lord with an everlasting salvation; you shall not be put to shame or confounded to all eternity.

¹⁸For thus says the Lord—Who created the heavens, God Himself, Who formed the earth and made it, Who established it and did not create it to be a worthless waste; He formed it to be inhabited—I am the Lord, and there is no one else.

¹⁹I have not spoken in secret, in a corner of the land of darkness; I did not call the descendants of Jacob [to a fruitless service], saying, Seek Me for nothing [but I promised them a just reward]. I, the Lord, speak righteousness (the truth—trustworthy, straightforward correspondence between deeds and words); I declare things that are right.

²⁰Assemble yourselves and come; draw near together, you survivors of the nations! They have no knowledge who carry about [in religious processions or into battle] their wooden idols and keep on praying to a god that cannot save.

²¹Declare and bring forward your strong arguments [for praying to gods that cannot save]; yes, take counsel together. Who announced this [the rise of Cyrus and his conquests] beforehand (long ago)? [What god] declared it of old? Was it not I, the Lord? And there is no other God besides Me, a rigidly and uncompromisingly just and righteous God and Savior; there is none besides Me.

²²Look to Me and be saved, all the ends of the earth! For I am God, and there is no other.

²³I have sworn by Myself, the word is gone out of My mouth in righteousness and shall not return, that unto Me every knee shall bow, every tongue shall swear [allegiance].

²⁴Only in the Lord shall one say, I have righteousness (salvation and victory) and strength [to achieve]. To Him shall all come who were incensed against Him, and they shall be ashamed.

²⁵In the Lord shall all the offspring of Israel be justified (enjoy righteousness, salvation, and victory) and shall be glorified.

Satan loves to work under a cover in darkness. He must have thought that God cannot see in the dark. But, since before time God has delighted to work in the dark. The fourth watch of the night, the watch just before dawn when the night is darkest is God's specialty. It was during the fourth watch of the night that Jesus walked on troubled water to comfort his frightened disciples.

God at work in the darkness is the pattern of creation. "In the beginning God created the heaven and the earth. And the earth was without form, and void; and darkness was upon the face of the deep. And the Spirit of God moved upon the face of the waters. And God said, Let there be light: and there was light" according to Genesis 1:1-3.

God's method of operation has always been to use people to accomplish His will. He wants to use you, as we read in the bible that he uses so many ordinary people and the only way he attend to those he uses was when they humble themselves and come to position themselves at their various birthing floor. Everyone that God uses, they position themselves for their breakthrough. What God is saying to you is, if you position yourself and get to the birthing floor and travail then he will hear and answer your prayer.

Your birthing floor can be your living room, at the altar in the Church, you prayer closet and I can keep the list going on and on.

Your birthing floor can be any place where God can meet with you, look at where he met with Saul.

Nowhere is this more clearly illustrated than in the conversion story of Saul of Tarsus. Saul was birthed out to Paul on the road to Damascus, God truly changed and delivered him in a new realm. God Himself stopped Saul on the road to Damascus; he heard the audible voice of God address him in the Hebrew language. He was left physically blind by this encounter with God, but when God sought to restore Saul's physical eyesight and open his spiritual eyesight, He worked through a man—Ananias. God instructed Saul," Arise, and go into the city, and it shall be told thee what thou must do" (Acts 9:6). God used Ananias to restore Saul's sight and to reveal the plan of salvation to Paul to baptize him in the name of Jesus Christ, and to pray for Saul as he received the Holy Ghost.

Now let me take you back to look at Mordecai and Esther. Mordecai possessed a deep faith for the Jewish people. He understood them to be God's people and was confident that God would deliver them from their present peril. In his challenge to Esther, he reminded her that the Jews would be delivered, whether or not she chose to become the source of deliverance.

Mordecai also understood that there is a tension between the sovereignty of God and the responsibility of man. He knew that God was in control, yet he also knew that God works through human agency. He made himself available to God. Mordecai did what he knew to do. He interceded for his people.

He donned sackcloth and ashes and took up residence outside the palace gate. When Esther received word of Mordecai's position, she was grieved and sent clothes to him to exchange for his sackcloth. When Mordecai refused to change, Esther summoned Hatach, the king's chamberlain assigned to her, and sent her to Mordecai to find out from him the source of his trouble. Mordecai informed Hatach of the decree of Haman against the Jews and he asked Esther to go to King Ahasuerus and request a reprieve for her people.

Esther was reluctant to approach Ahasuerus. Only those called to come before the King were welcomed to enter the throne room. To go into the room without being called ment death, unless the king extended his golden scepter to the visitor. Esther dispatched Hatach to tell Mordecai of her quandary. Mordecai refused to accept Esther's excuse and challenged her to take the risk. He said that she had no choice but to go before Ahasuerus. He explained to her that neither she nor her family would escape the coming genocide. But he did more than motivate her by fear. He inspired Esther.

Mordecai recognized the providential hand of God in the placement of Esther in the palace of the king. His words challenged her deeply: "Who knoweth whether thou art come to the kingdom for such a time as this?" Esther 4:14. Mordecai understood that God was in control and the unlikely choice of Esther as queen now made sense. Esther was the key to the salvation of the Jews.

God often triumphs over situations by using people. He used Moses to lead the people of Israel out of Egyptian captivity. He used Gideon to defeat the Midianites who were stealing Israel's crops and their courage. He used David to destroy the giant, Goliath, and the giant of fear. Each of these men arrived on the scene just in time. Moses labored for forty years for his father-in-law until God changed his job description. Gideon threshed wheat under the cover of darkness until the Lord called him to lead Israel. David tended his father's sheep until his time came. Each in his own way turned the tide against the enemies of God's people. God maneuvered them into their place in the kingdom when He needed them.

Mordecai's stiff challenge caused Esther to evaluate her position in the king's household. At first glance, it looked like she had much to lose. If she appeared uninvited before King Ahasuerus, she risked death. The memory of Queen Vashti's humiliation was fresh in Esther's mind. However, the annihilation of her people was more than she could bear. The Jews were more than just her people; they were God's children. Somehow God would come through for them, and for her.

Esther is the heroine of this story, but we must never underestimate the role of Mordecai. He encouraged Esther, but he did more than encourage her; he challenged her to become involved. His pointed remarks and unflinching courage motivated her to appear before the king with her request. Without Mordecai's support it is doubtful that Esther would have taken the risk of losing her life.

Esther, strengthened by Mordecai's encouragement, sought and was granted an audience with King Ahasuerus. She invited him—and Haman—to a banquet she was preparing in the king's honor. When the king asked Esther if she had a request, she invited him and Haman to another banquet. Haman's head grew larger with each invitation. He was encouraged by his wife Zeresh and his friends to order a gallows be constructed for the fly in the ointment of his life—Mordecai.

At the second banquet, the king again asked Esther if she had a request he could grant. Esther revealed to King Ahasuerus the plot against her and her people. The king was enraged and demanded to know who had hatched this plot. Esther replied that Haman was her adversary and enemy. The king hanged Haman on the gallows that Haman had constructed to execute Mordecai.

Since the king could not revoke his previous decree that threatened the life of the Jewish people, King Ahasuerus devised a way for the Jews to defend themselves against their enemies. So the Jews were successful in defending themselves and destroying their enemies.

God will always make a way when there's no way. What is impossible for God to do? There is nothing in heaven or on earth that is impossible for him to do. It is very important that you know God has given you the will power to break forth and come forth with power and might. Who can push you through better than yourself, God wants to do it but you have to journey it through to come through.

CHAPTER FIVE

THE BIRTHING OF PASSIONATE PRAYER

Confess to one another therefore your faults (your slips, your false steps, your offenses, your sins) and pray [also] for one another, that you may be healed and restored [to a spiritual tone of mind and heart]. The earnest (heartfelt, continued) prayer of a righteous man makes tremendous power available [dynamic in its working]. James 5:16 (Amplified Bible)

How can one actually be empowered to function in the full capacity of their God given gifts and ability or to experience full breakthrough in the midst of difficult situations and circumstances. It is important to take a look at some of the great generals in Christ who have walk this journey before us and how they make it through. And that is through prayers; especially we can see this in the life of Abraham, Moses, the apostle Paul and our personal Lord and Savior Jesus Christ.

In this chapter of the Birthing floor I want us to focus on prayer. It takes prayer to move the hand of God. Most times we focus on our problems and situation and how to handle or deal with it by reading books or asking advise from others, seeking professional help, instead of bringing it before God to help us through it. There are times when the definition of prayer can be misinterpreted. Prayer is not just talking to God, but it involves listening also. Prayer is communication, and a one-way conversation does not last long. When you pray, expect God to speak to you.

Most often He will do this through His written Word or by a "still small voice" that seems to "speak" to your heart. Sometimes He will give you a vision or interpret back to your spirit what you have prayed in your heavenly prayer language. Don't just rush in and dump all your requests on God and then end your prayer. Allow time for Him to speak to you. He will give answers to your questions, guidance for the day ahead, and help you order your priorities. Sometimes He will give you a special message of encouragement to share with someone for whom you are interceding. I have personally come to a place in my life where I thoroughly depend on prayer not that I am ruling out help or advise but as the scripture says unless the Lord builds a house the laborer builds in vain.

Prayer is very important in every aspects of life. It keeps you in right relationship with God and let Satan know that you are right with God. It was a Sunday night after preaching in three Holy Ghost filled miracle services and then traveled to attend a week of conference. Just after praying thoughts of what had happened in these services were tumbled out one after another as I tried to fall asleep in a hotel room in Bloomfield, Connecticut. My wife Veronica and others had just left me at a hotel in Bloomfield, Connecticut and traveled back home to New York. It was about 12:45AM a harsh banging was on the room door and I jumped, it was like someone had kicked and forcefully pushed open the door.

Seconds after my eyes were wide open while still lying on the bed trying to figure out where the banging came from, it was to my surprise all of a sudden I saw this big huge dark shadow standing over me with a tumbling voice saying "I was waiting for you to be alone for a long time now" I began to tremble and the worst of fear by then had gripped my heart trying to make believe that its only a dream.

As I was trying to make believe it was only a dream, I was trying to figure out what to do in this moment of despair. Again I heard this ugly thundering voice shouted again "I am here to kill you" at this time my body became so heavy that I could not even lift my fingers, much less my hands. A thought came to mind to get up and jump through the room windows but my body was so heavy that I could not do anything at the time.

As I began to see the shadow begin to move closer to me I heard a still small voice speak into my ears with authority and strength saying "Tell him I am here and you are not alone" at that time all of a sudden my mouth got strength again and I shouted "Devil I am not alone Jesus is with me" the shout has caught the attention of people next door and in minutes as the hotel security came up to the room asking what was wrong. I felt the heaviness from my body leave and I was able to get up and pray thanking the Lord for intervening.

I shared this story to say this that not only Satan will know when you pray that you have a relationship with God it also reminds him that prayer is what keeps the armor of God on you so that you can withstand the plans of the devil; prayer keeps you close to God while it also brings God close to you. Having constant conversation with God is very important; I thought to myself what if I didn't pray before I tried to sleep or what if I was not in constant communicating with Him. Communicating with God through your prayer is essential. Prayer makes a difference no matter what the situation is. There is power in prayer, it can change this world, it bothers the devil, shakes nations, move foundations, saves souls, brings revival and brings you out of any storms in life. When you have the armor of God and stay focused on God the enemy cannot have power over you. The bible says in Ephesians 6:11-18

[11]Put on God's whole armor [the armor of a heavy-armed soldier which God supplies], that you may be able successfully to stand up against [all] the strategies and the deceits of the devil.

[12]For we are not wrestling with flesh and blood [contending only with physical opponents], but against the despotisms, against the powers, against [the master spirits who are] the world rulers of this present darkness, against the spirit forces of wickedness in the heavenly (supernatural) sphere.

¹³Therefore put on God's complete armor, that you may be able to resist and stand your ground on the evil day [of danger], and, having done all [the crisis demands], to stand [firmly in your place].

¹⁴Stand therefore [hold your ground], having tightened the belt of truth around your loins and having put on the breastplate of integrity and of moral rectitude and right standing with God,

¹⁵And having shod your feet in preparation [to face the enemy with the firm-footed stability, the promptness, and the readiness produced by the good news] of the Gospel of peace.

¹⁶Lift up over all the [covering] shield of saving faith, upon which you can quench all the flaming missiles of the wicked [one].

¹⁷And take the helmet of salvation and the sword that the Spirit wields, which is the Word of God.

¹⁸Pray at all times (on every occasion, in every season) in the Spirit, with all [manner of] prayer and entreaty. To that end keep alert and watch with strong purpose and perseverance, interceding in behalf of all the saints (God's consecrated people).

Anything could have happened to me that night if my life was not in constant contact with God through prayer and having the armor of God covering me. Always remember that you can have the covering of God if you keep in constant connection with him. You have the opportunity to approach the throne of grace when anything goes wrong in your life. Don't you ever feel like you cannot approach the throne of God because the bible says when the enemy comes in like a flood God will raise a standard.

God wants to provide covering to his people and because the scripture says he is able and just to forgive us of all our sins and inequities. And that is because he loves us and wants us to communicate with him. If ever you will break forth and give birth you must bring your prayer life in alignment.

If you look at Jabez and what his life was and what it is after he prayed; Jabez name means sorrow his mother named him Jabez because he was born out of sorrow but Jabez refused to accept the very position his life was in and so he repositioned himself and made demand on heaven for a change.

Prayer is making demand on heaven and you have the right to pray and make demand on heaven just like Hannah did as I talked about earlier. Let me show you what Jabez did. The scriptures say that Jabez prayed and made three requests.

In the book of 1 Chronicles 4:10 Jabez cried to the God of Israel, saying, Oh, that You would bless me and enlarge my border, and that Your hand might be with me, and You would keep me from evil so it might not hurt me! And God granted his request.

Here is where Jabez gave birth to the four things that he requested from God through prayer the first thing was blessings, Jabez asks God to bless him and so he gave birth to blessings; you have the right to ask God for a blessing. God promised to bless those who fear and love him, the second thing he asked God for, is that God would enlarge his territory or increase his responsibility and so he gave birth to increase such a capacity, you also have the right to ask God to enlarge your territory, God's word promised to enlarge us just make your request known to him, the third thing he asked for was that God will be with him and stay close and so God did, you can ask God to provide his guidance and protect you from every fiery darts of the enemy, the bible says he will gave his angel charge over thee, and lastly Jabez asks that God would keep him in perfect peace and from harm so that he will be free from pain and so he gave birth to peace and new strength with no pain. The bible says the joy of the Lord is your strength.

This prayer of Jabez reveals that Jabez understands what many believers don't understand and that is, God is the only one that can take away the very pain that anyone is suffering. Always remember mental, emotional and spiritual pains can never be treated by a doctor, a counselor or medication but only God through prayer. According to the scriptures in Philippians 4:6 it says "do not fret or have any anxiety about anything, but in every circumstance and in everything, by prayer and petition definite requests, with thanksgiving, continue to make your wants known to God.

It is important that you make the choice to allow God into your life through the power of prayer and make your petition for his blessings and guidance so that you can birth out everything that he promised you. Jabez wants to succeed and increase his sphere of influence for God. The specific sphere of influence is not important. What is important is that when we want to reach for goals and accomplishments that you have God on your side. I personally know without any doubts that it is God's blessings and the fulfillment of his promises that make me the person who I am today. Just as Proverbs 16:3 says, "Commit thy works unto the LORD, and thy thoughts shall be established." It is critical to understand and practice this in a close relationship with God.

Further, it is equally important to stay close to God and rely on His continued support and guidance throughout life. Jabez clearly knows and prays specifically to the One who can protect him from evil and pain and that is God. At the end of the verse it is clear that God approved of this faithful prayer by granting it. It is also important to see that Jabez was passionate in his plea to God: "He cried out to the God of Israel." God wants to hear that we need Him through passionate prayer.

Passionate prayer will bring about a greater release for you. You can read in the book of Daniel chapter 9 verses 1-23 that Daniel's prayer is full of passion, both outwardly and inwardly. Daniel prays earnestly, fasting, and dressed in sackcloth and ashes. This shows how his whole being is involved with his prayer. We don't tend to give a great deal of attention to our bodily posture when we pray these days. But we are embodied creatures, and our bodies affect the way we feel and what we do. When we raise our heads and our arms, we feel more thankful; when we kneel or prostrate ourselves, we feel more humble and penitent. When we dance, we feel joyful. Daniel's prayer reminds us that our prayers can be fuelled and reinforced by what we do with our bodies. And when we pray in private, as Jesus taught us to do, and there's no chance of disturbing others (as Paul warned us against) perhaps we can think about how what we do with our bodies can help our prayer.

Daniel's passion is not just demonstrated by his outward behaviors. It infuses all that he says. His prayer is passionate in praise. He reviews God's mighty acts in Israel's history, and recounts his faithfulness to the covenant. He praises God's power and constancy, mercy, love and forgiveness. His prayer begins, continues and ends with worship. Does our prayer begin, continue and end like this?

Daniel's prayer was also passionate in penitence. He reviews in great detail the ways in which his people have failed in their commitment to the covenant and rebelled against and ignored God and the prophets. There are some people who are passionate about penitence in the wrong way, constantly talking themselves down, and in the process, convincing themselves that they are so weak and so evil that they absolve themselves of any responsibility to make any difference to the situation. Daniel shows proper, realistic, responsible penitence; he doesn't do what we so often do – blame everyone else, but absolve ourselves. Daniel (who is a good man we are told) accepts and confesses his own part in the sins of his people, and asks forgiveness and mercy for himself, as well as for all the previous and present members of the exiled Jewish community. Do we do this when we pray? Or is our passion reserved for blaming others, especially others in the church, for what we perceive to have gone wrong?

Lastly, Daniel is passionate in pleading. He intercedes for his people, and asks God to release them from their enslavement to an alien culture. This was the situation both in the time in which the Book of Daniel was written, when the Jews were ruled by the mad Seleucid Emperor, Antiochus Epiphanes; and of the time described in the book, when many of the leading Jews were in exile in Babylon. Daniel knows what he believes God ought to do, and he pleads for it with every fiber in his body.

I suspect that if we are ever passionate in prayer, it is in intercession. Which of us has not at some time prayed passionately to God for ourselves or others – for someone gravely ill, or recovering from a disaster, for good news of a loved one, for someone facing a situation they don't think they can cope with. Just as how the book of Luke said it, Luke chapter 11 verses 2-13 says:

And He said to them, When you pray, say: Our Father Who is in heaven, hallowed be Your name, Your kingdom come. Your will be done [held holy and revered] on earth as it is in heaven.

³Give us daily our bread food for the morrow].

⁴And forgive us our sins, for we ourselves also forgive everyone who is indebted to us [who has offended us or done us wrong]. And bring us not into temptation but rescue us from evil.

⁵And He said to them, Which of you who has a friend will go to him at midnight and will say to him, Friend, lend me three loaves [of bread],

⁶For a friend of mine who is on a journey has just come, and I have nothing to put before him;

⁷And he from within will answer, Do not disturb me; the door is now closed, and my children are with me in bed; I cannot get up and supply you [with anything]?

⁸I tell you, although he will not get up and supply him anything because he is his friend, yet because of his shameless persistence and insistence he will get up and give him as much as he needs.

⁹So I say to you, Ask and keep on asking and it shall be given you; seek and keep on seeking and you shall find; knock and keep on knocking and the door shall be opened to you.

¹⁰For everyone who asks and keeps on asking receives; and he who seeks and keeps on seeking finds; and to him who knocks and keeps on knocking, the door shall be opened.

¹¹What father among you, if his son asks for a loaf of bread, will give him a stone; or if he asks for a fish, will instead of a fish give him a serpent?

¹²Or if he asks for an egg, will give him a scorpion?

¹³If you then, evil as you are, know how to give good gifts [gifts that are to their advantage] to your children, how much more will your heavenly Father give the Holy Spirit to those who ask and continue to ask Him!

Does the passion with which you pray make any difference to God's response? Does prayer operate like Opportunity Knocks, Bob Barker's game show the price is right, where the contestant had to know a retail price and bid to come close to the actual retail price of the item in order for them to stand a chance of winning and thus achieving their heart's desire?

The story of Daniel indicates that this is not the case with God, who responds in a way that is consistent with his character, with mercy and justice, no matter how people pray. God doesn't give in to Daniel's passionate pleas – but he does explain to him what is to come for his people, and why.

So is there any point in passionate prayer? Yes, because the depth of passion we put into our prayers – whether it is passion in its meaning of suffering, or emotion, or love – is a measure of how deeply we are committed to aligning our will to God's will, and conforming our nature to God's will. The more that happens, the more God can use our prayers to achieve his purpose to bring us in alignment and birth us out and placed our blessings in our hands.

Passionate Prayer brings you into the Presence of God:

It is very important to know that when you go into prayer it is going into God's presence, so before you enter into your closet to pray you must always recognize that it is a very sacred moment and that place will become holy because you are going into the presence of the King. And just as how there is a certain protocol in entering a secular Kings presence, there is also certain protocol in entering into the King of Kings presence.

The birthing floor is all about the presence of God. And if you take a close look at the Lords prayer Jesus taught us how to conduct ourselves and pray when we are in the presence of the King. In the book of Matthew chapter six Jesus taught some very important things about prayer and mainly gives a role model prayer. He said after this manner therefore pray ye: Our father which art in heaven, Hallowed be thy name. Thy kingdom come. Thy will be done in earth, as it is in heaven. Give us this day our daily bread. And forgive us our debts, as we forgive our debtors. And lead us not into temptation, but deliver us from evil: For thine is the kingdom, and the power, and the glory, for ever. Amen.

Now this is a way or structure of how Jesus taught us to pray, he explains each part of the model prayer to us and gave his own commentary on each part. When he says "in heaven" he was referring to the presence of God or the abode of God. Matthew 6:19-23 talk about "in heaven", Heaven is the abode of God; let us place our hearts and desires towards the things of heaven, and not on the earth as Jesus said. When you begin to pray, get your priorities straight. You must be one who seeks the things of Heaven more than the things on earth. The bible says seek ye first the kingdom of God and his righteousness and all these things shall be added unto you.

It is very important to have a proper attitude when you are in the presence of God. That is why Jesus said Hallowed be thy name. Start praying by worshiping God and getting your heart in reverence and one accord with Him. If ever you are going to give birth to greatness your heart must have the right motive and attitude for the things of God. Jesus also talked about "Our Father" in Matthew 6:11-12 Jesus explains here that when you begin to pray, understand that your father knows that you have needs. Jesus encourages us that God loves us so much, because He is our Father, and that you ought to pray in faith, believing that He will give you what you need. The bible says that God will not withhold anything good from them that loves him. In fact, Jesus said in Matthew 6:25 and 28, why do we take thought for raiment and food? God knows we have these needs.

So Jesus is saying that when we seek needs, make them spiritual needs, God is going to take care of your clothing and food without you having to tell him. When you were a kid did you ever say "daddy,

I think you ought to buy me some food and new clothing for school because school is reopening" No your parents knew then that you have those needs. So Jesus is saying to you today have some faith that He is our Father, and pray for spiritual needs. In Matthew 6:10 Jesus taught us to pray "Thy kingdom come" this is the first request you should always pray for because as I mentioned before Jesus said seek first the kingdom of God because he knows what's your physical needs are Matthew 6:33-34. So don't seek things, but seek first the kingdom of God, and then these other things will automatically be added to you. Why because God knows you have need of these things. And if you ask what is the Kingdom of God? Well Romans 14:17 describe the things of the kingdom of God and this is righteousness, peace and joy amongst one another in the Holy Ghost.

It is very important to seek after the will of God, if ever you are going to experience that answer to your prayers follow what Jesus said in Matthew 7:1-6. Whenever the will of God is referred to without explaining exactly what that will is, generally speaking, it is what Matthew 22:37-40 said.

Love God with all your heart and your neighbor as yourself. So next you must begin to pray that God's will be done in you, if you examine Adam he was made of earth, in earth. And that is the reason Jesus speaks of judging not and not giving holy things to dogs, or people who will only mock you. If you love God then you will love people. If you cannot love people, how can you say you love God. John 4:7-8 said

Prayer is making your request known to God. Jesus said in the model prayer "Give us this day our daily Bread" Jesus explains what this means in Matthew 7:7-11. He distinctly mentions that when you ask you shall receive, it's this simple God will supply all your needs according to the riches in Glory this is what his word said. And his word will not return void to him, as you continued in prayer ask God to increase your faith at the point where you can see it even though it is not into reality as yet, to again receive what you pray for.

Previously I said, Jesus said that you do not need to pray for clothes and food, but here He says there is something you must pray for, but when you pray, believe you will get it and so shall it be.

Pray with faith when you enter the presence of God. Mark 11:24 says if you pray you will receive. Since we are praying to Our Father, Jesus said that which father of you would give a stone to his son who asked for bread. This shows that if you would give bread, then how much more will your father give you? Compared to God, your love for your children is a shadow. Ask for things believing that you will get them, this is very important.

Forgiveness is very important whenever you enter into God's presence. Jesus talked about this in Matthew 7:12

The model prayer taught how to pray by saying "Forgive us our debts as we forgive our debtors" The model prayer tells us that we can only pray to be forgiven if we will forgive others. This is exactly what Jesus says here, whatever you want men to do to you or whatever you want God to do for you, then do it to them first. If you want God to forgive you, then you must forgive those who hurt you or does things against you. It is very important to know that if you want to be treated mercifully by God, then you must treat others mercifully. If you're mistaken and want people to understand you did not mean to do a wrong, then you better have understanding and realize that perhaps people did not mean to do you wrong when they did you wrong.

In closing this chapter on passionate prayer of the Birthing Floor let me say this; obeying God's word is very important in your life. Jesus ends the model prayer by saying "For thine is the Kingdom and the power and the Glory forever, Amen" meaning obeying his words is important. In other words, you must pray His way because you want to enter his eternal kingdom in glory one day. You are in the Kingdom now, but you want to appear with Him when He comes again, so Jesus was talking about people who will not enter. He speaks of those who did many wonderful works in His name and does not deny they were genuine miracles, but disobey. Jesus says that he will deny those, He knows the thoughts of all souls.

There are people who do things that are great and mighty, these are people who were doing things in the name of Jesus without having a Relationship with him. They did things in their own way. That is why Jesus says that the one who hears these sayings of him and does them, is like a wise man building a house on a rock. What saying? The very structure he put in place on how to pray as you enter with passion into his presence.

If you pray the way Jesus prescribes, then you cover all the bases, and that is when you prayed first make sure heaven is your priority then pray in faith to God as your Father who will give you your necessities, also seeking spiritual things of God above all other things, the fourth thing you should do is seeking to love God and your neighbor as yourself, the fifth thing you should pray for is faith for whatsoever you ask for, and continued prayer for forgiveness, forgiving others so you can be forgiven, then recognizing false doctrine so as not to be deceived. You will never fail if you pray for these things, you will be like a man building his house on a rock that stands against storms, you will not be like those who think they are saved just because they pray for healing but never think to have a relationship with God and do things their own way. Just remember many will go before God thinking they did just fine, but will find out they should have thought to seek God and learn his ways.

CHAPTER SIX

THE PLACE OF CONSECRATION

But it is from Him that you have your life in Christ Jesus, Whom God made our Wisdom from God, [revealed to us a knowledge of the divine plan of salvation previously hidden, manifesting itself as] our Righteousness [thus making us upright and putting us in right standing with God], and our Consecration [making us pure and holy], and our Redemption [providing our ransom from eternal penalty for sin]. 1 Corinthians 1:30 (Amplified Bible)

What is consecration? Consecration is the voluntary dedication of one's self to God during a specific period of time where fasting and prayers are being done, an offering definitely made, and made without any reservation whatsoever. It is the setting apart of all that you are, all that you have, and all that you expect to have or to be, to God first and utmost. It is not so much the giving of yourself to the Church or ministry, or the mere engaging in some line of church work. But giving yourself to God the almighty and Jesus who is the Savior of the World who is in view and is the end of all consecration. It is a separation of flesh from the spirit man, a devotion fully to God for his sacred use.

Consecration is very important and plays a great role in the aspect of your walk with God as a believer. It is the physical side of separating yourselves from every sin. Paul writings in the book of

Hebrews 12:1-2 says "Therefore, since we are surrounded by such a great cloud of witnesses, let us throw off everything that hinders and the sin that so easily entangles, and let us run with perseverance the race marked out for us. Let us fix our eyes on Jesus, the author and perfecter of our faith, who for the joy set before him endured the cross, scorning its shame, and sat down at the right hand of the throne of God. ³Consider him who endured such opposition from sinful men, so that you will not grow weary and lose heart."

God wants to use you for his honor and glory and choose you to do his work; he wants to prepare you for his use by actually making you holy, just as his word says "be ye holy for I am holy". That is to say prepare yourselves for holiness because he wants to bless you with the purity of heart, body, mind and spirit before he can use you and increase you. It is very important to known that God started the cleansing process in your life by first washing you with the cleansing blood of his son Jesus Christ. This process started from the very moment you acknowledged Jesus Christ as your personal Lord and Savior.

When you acknowledge him he cleansed you on the inside and made you holy. After salvation, God consecrated us for his use by washing your body with his presence. So for God to super impose his anointing on you that you can experience the fullness of his benefits you must come to a place of holiness. If ever God will use you or entrust you with greatness and blessings you must come to a place of consecration.

Jesus said in the book of John 17:6-21 I have manifested Your Name [I have revealed Your very Self, Your real Self] to the people whom You have given Me out of the world. They were Yours, and You gave them to Me, and they have obeyed and kept Your word.

Now [at last] they know and understand that all You have given Me belongs to You [is really and truly Yours].

For the [uttered] words that You gave Me I have given them; and they have received and accepted [them] and have come to know positively and in reality [to believe with absolute assurance] that I came forth from Your presence, and they believed and are convinced that You did send Me.

I am praying for them. I am not praying (requesting) for the world, but for those You have given Me, for they belong to You.

All [things that are] Mine are Yours, and all [things that are] Yours belong to Me; and I am glorified in (through) them. [They have done Me honor; in them My glory is achieved.]

And [now] I am no more in the world, but these are [still] in the world, and I am coming to You. Holy Father, keep in Your Name [in the knowledge of Yourself] those whom You have given Me, that they may be one as We [are one].

While I was with them, I kept and preserved them in Your Name [in the knowledge and worship of You]. Those You have given Me I guarded and protected, and not one of them has perished or is lost except the son of perdition [Judas Iscariot—the one who is now doomed to destruction, destined to be lost], that the Scripture might be fulfilled.

13And now I am coming to You; I say these things while I am still in the world, so that My joy may be made full and complete and perfect in them [that they may experience My delight fulfilled in them, that My enjoyment may be perfected in their own souls, that they may have My gladness within them, filling their hearts].

14I have given and delivered to them Your word (message) and the world has hated them, because they are not of the world [do not belong to the world], just as I am not of the world.

15I do not ask that You will take them out of the world, but that You will keep and protect them from the evil one.

16They are not of the world (worldly, belonging to the world), [just] as I am not of the world.

17Sanctify them [purify, consecrate, separate them for Yourself, make them holy] by the Truth; Your Word is Truth.

¹⁸Just as You sent Me into the world, I also have sent them into the world.

¹⁹And so for their sake and on their behalf I sanctify (dedicate, consecrate) Myself, that they also may be sanctified (dedicated, consecrated, made holy) in the Truth.

²⁰Neither for these alone do I pray [it is not for their sake only that I make this request], but also for all those who will ever come to believe in (trust in, cling to, rely on) Me through their word and teaching,

²¹That they all may be one, [just] as You, Father, are in Me and I in You, that they also may be one in us, so that the world may believe and be convinced that You have sent Me.

Many people wanted to be used by God, but don't want to consecrate themselves before God. No one is righteous enough to approach the throne of God without consecrating themselves first. In the Old Testament before God uses anyone they first had to go through consecration. God is a holy God and if ever you want to experience his anointing you must actually draw near to him. God designed and created you to be drawn close to him but sin has caused the separation between you and God but that can only change through forgiveness and consecration. So you are designed to draw close to God and by drawing close to God, purity works and forgiveness work its way into your experience because enjoying God's presence becomes your preferred way of quenching, not sin or unwanted behaviors.

Drawing to God will automatically decrease the earthly ways of unrighteous living because less and less the world will have anything to offer you when God started to fill you up with his presence. Turning to God and drawing close to him it will cause things to happen; your life will change, you will begin to see things differently. By drawing near to God and you letting Him draw near to you, it will enable you to be prepared for his use because he washes you with holiness all the while he is drawing near to you. Ask yourself this question. Do I really want to be prepared for God's purposes? You have to draw near to God and let him draw near to you, or the outside of your vessel won't be consecrated to God. God is willing and able to do his part. You just have to be prepared to do yours.

Consecration must come before your prayer, worship, praise and intercession. 2 Chronicles 29:31 says Then Hezekiah said, now you have consecrated yourselves to the Lord; come near and bring sacrifices and thank offerings into the house of the Lord. And the assembly brought in sacrifices and thank offerings, and as many as were of a willing heart brought burnt offerings.

The cross of Christ is the pathway to experiencing the presence of God. You have to consecrate yourselves before you can enter the throne room to draw near to the Lord. But you must remember that consecration is not something that you can do and then think you are done with it. The bible also says in Luke 14:27 whoever does not persevere and carry his own cross and come after (follow) me cannot be my disciple. So carrying your cross is something that you will always have to do. No one will ever grow enough to put their cross down. Second Corinthians 4:10 says Always carrying about in the body the liability and exposure to the same putting to death that the Lord Jesus suffered, so that the [resurrection] life of Jesus also may be shown forth by and in our bodies. Here is where the Apostle Paul talks about always caring about the dying of Jesus. Since we won't ever grow out of it, consecration has to become a way of life.

Just remember that your consecration would never be complete. So when it says, "now that you have consecrated yourselves to the Lord, come near according to 2 Chronicle 29:31, this does not mean that you should be fully consecrated before you draw near to God. So don't wait for the day when you look at your practical righteousness and say, "Now I think I am doing good enough to draw near." If you do that, you will only be depending on the righteousness you think you have achieved and not God.

Be in consecration for several days or just a few weeks and then take steps to draw near to God. Sin has a contaminating effect on everything around it; you deceive yourselves if you imagine that you can come before God and please Him in any way apart from first consecrating yourselves. In fact God has made it clear that He will not bless rituals and religious activity or even sacrificial offerings or an energetic prayer warrior that does not flow out of a life that has first been consecrated to Him. But the encouraging message is that God has committed Himself to bless the service of those who put a priority on holiness. We might not see the abundant fruit immediately; but as you are patient and persevere, God will abundantly bless you. There is a direct connection between obedience and God's blessing.

So I personally recommend seventy-two hours which is three days before God in consecration; the number three speaks of the "DBR" the death of Christ, meaning you need to put sin to death in your life before you approach the throne of God. Secondly the burial of Christ, meaning that sins needs to be buried and thrown away as far as possible from us and lastly the resurrection of Jesus, coming forth, rising up be renewed and ready to go up, meaning coming out of uncleanness and now being clean before God and ready to rise up in righteousness and prepare to approach his throne and meet with him.

When you enter and finish consecration you become dedicated, you become set apart, you are going to experience something special from God himself. You will definitely feel clean and ready. What an amazing privilege you have, God wants you to be ready for him. For Israel consecration involves some ritual things. It involved a ritual washing of themselves, a ritual washing of their clothes. They lived in a country where water was scarce, so they weren't bathing every day; so bathing and washing clothes was a pretty high deal. And so, it was viewed as sort of a symbolic moment of starting in a new direction, in a new stage of life even. You see that in the New Testament where it talks about cleansing and water and putting on new clothes as being a symbol of living a new life. It was part of their mindset. So they would symbolically wash in this anticipation that something is going to be different; something is going to change.

Changes had to happen on a heart level. It's not just a ritual, it's the heart. The children of Israel had to put their attention on God. They had to draw close. They had to pay attention. They had to be available. They had to be ready, because God was coming to do something. Always remember that getting ready for God is not a casual thing. When you consecrate yourselves before God you can expect great things to happen. So as you enter into your personal birthing floor believe that God is going to be working with you for a change. Just as Joshua told the people "consecrate yourselves, for tomorrow the Lord will do amazing things among you." So in return I say God is going to do amazing things in your life as you consecrate yourself. I am convinced of it, not because you are worthy, not because you are skilled or because you are great, but because it's your time now. You are living in a time when God is going to do something in you as you get ready. When you consecrate yourself before God you will see God's grace and power in ways that you haven't seen before. Your lives will be changed and potentials will be increased in you. Your life will be changed as you engage with God in this. And what's most important and most exciting is in new and deeper ways Christ will be worshipped and obeyed and God will do this, not you, but you do have a responsibility to consecrate yourself, to be prepared, available, ready to be used when this happens, to be in the right place facing in the right direction with your eyes and hearts open, ready to respond, ready to follow, ready for someone special. Consecrate yourselves, for tomorrow the Lord will do amazing things among you.

Always remember as you consecrate yourself, you will become more in tune with what God is saying to you. You will get a clearer perspective on your lives and on your circumstances. You will become more aware of the sin and darkness that is in you and around you. You will become more like Jesus and begin to flow in spiritual gifts that you normally don't flow in. You will begin to receive visions and experience God in different ways, at higher levels. Henri Nouwen said it best in his book, the way of the heart, He said "Solitude, silence, and unceasing prayer form the core concepts of the spirituality of the desert." When you consecrate yourself, transformation occurs.

When you consecrate yourself before God expect things to happen, consecration will birth you into position for a great change. That change will birth favor in your life, and favor will birth blessings and blessings will birth your dreams and vision in your spirit and bring it into reality.

In closing this chapter of the birthing floor just purpose in your heart before you continue to read this book to start seventy-two hours of consecration. Follow the following pattern for a successful seventy-two hours of consecration.

Preparation for Consecration:

The first thing you must do is to set aside the days you want to start your period of consecration with fasting and prayer. After setting aside the days, plan what activities you will be involved in during this time of consecration, then prepare yourself physically and emotionally for this sacred time with God.

It is very important to prepare yourself physically and emotionally. Make a vow to God that you will fast and consecrate yourself for his service. Recognize your limitations and admit that you cannot break your habit alone. Allow friends, family and prayer partners help you defeat your habit. Go to a place where you can meet God, your birthing floor can be a silent room, your church altar etc.

Consecration is very sacred and sometimes it is necessary to celebrate the fast and consecration in secret. Get into a secret place with God and revisit the place of past spiritual victories. Revisit the place symbolically in your memory. Focus on your consecration and fast to hear the Word of the Lord. During this time study to know what the Bible says, not what you think it says. Depressed people need to receive a positive external influence from outside their thinking. Allow the Word of God to reveal your weakness.

When you read the Word of God, begin to question where you are spiritually. Only when you question your habitual thought patterns can the bondage of mental habits be broken. During the fast and consecration use scripture as a mirror to show you your weaknesses where you are emotionally and spiritually, confess and agree with God about your weakness.

When you are filled with self justification, you cannot confess your needs. So don't cover your need with the claim to be defending God he can defend himself. Look for Quiet, Inner meaning because habits are broken not by external forces, but from within. Your strength comes from within as you build up the inner person in Christ Jesus

It is important to look within the Word of God, and listen with your own inner ear to hear what the Lord is saying to you. During this time look for the positive through God's eyes. As long as you focus on your problems, you will exercise faith in your problems. Don't focus on your problems focus on your cleansing through the blood of Jesus Christ. God wants us to focus on His power so we can have more faith in His power rather than in our problems.

In consecration plan positive and Godly actions, the way to break a bad habit is to acquire a stronger positive habit. It is good to develop the ability to see yourselves as you really are, but more importantly, to develop the ability to see yourselves as God sees you.

Prepare to see potential results. People break bad habits when they have goals that are stronger than the attractions of their bad habits. When you understand your importance in God's plan, you can leave your despondency behind.

Remember these five Principles during your moment of Consecration.

1. Focus on the Biblical principles of strength developed by withdrawing to "a place of rest," as Elijah did during fasting and prayer.
2. Always have your Bible and other study tools with you because during your consecration God can give you mighty revelations.
3. Fast and pray for God to give you a positive self-image mirroring Biblical character.
4. Consecrate yourself through fasting and prayer for the positive actions God would have you do.
5. Develop a list of prayer requests for times of consecration and fasting. List all the habits and things you want God to cleanse you from.

Be encouraged as you read the word of God during your time of Consecration. The following Scriptures from the Word of God are highly recommended.

Numbers chapter 13 & 14, Matthew chapter 6 and Isaiah 58:15, Book of Romans for dealing with the sin nature. Book of John, Book of Hebrews, Book of Proverbs, John 15, Ephesians 4 and 5, Romans 13 and I Corinthians 12 and 13.

During your period of consecration and fasting, it is highly recommended that you follow this list.

Recommendation for liquid fast "Use in moderation"
1. Water
2. Milk
3. Naturally pure vegetable juices
4. Grape juices
5. Apple juices
6. Orange juices
7. Tea (in moderation no sugar)
8. Any type of natural fruit juice

If you are partaking in the working fast "Use in moderation"
1. Raw vegetables (carrots, celery, spinach, etc)
2. Fruit: Bananas, apples, strawberries, etc.
3. Some meal replacement supplements

Prayer of Consecration and sanctification

Father I come to you in the precious name of our Lord and Savior Jesus Christ who died on the cross of Calvary for all my sins and iniquity according to your word.

As your soul who you saved from sin and iniquity I covenant with you Jesus, to seek you first, to love you with all of my heart and other fellow man as myself. I declare that I will serve you with gladness and joyfulness just as your word said in Matthew 6:33 But seek (aim at and strive after) first of all His kingdom and His righteousness (His way of doing and being right), and then all these things taken together will be given you besides.

Also as your word says in Matthew 22:37 And He replied to him, You shall love the Lord your God with all your heart and with all your soul and with all your mind (intellect).

I will give you praise and honor in my life and in my services. I declare that I will represent you appropriately by living in holiness and in abundance by effectively using the dominion and authority you have given me for living.

I declare I shall be led by Your Holy Spirit and function in the gifts and callings that You have divided to me through the Holy Spirit to be profit to you and your body, Lord Jesus. Just as Psalm 145:5 says On the glorious splendor of Your majesty and on Your wondrous works I will meditate, Genesis 1:28 And God blessed them and said to them, Be fruitful, multiply, and fill the earth, and subdue it [using all its vast resources in the service of God and man]; and have dominion over the fish of the sea, the birds of the air, and over every living creature that moves upon the earth.

Matthew 28:18-20 Jesus approached and, breaking the silence, said to them, All authority (all power of rule) in heaven and on earth has been given to Me. Go then and make disciples of all the nations, baptizing them into the name of the Father and of the Son and of the Holy Spirit, Teaching them to observe everything that I have commanded you, and behold, I am with you all the days (perpetually, uniformly, and on every occasion), to the [very] close and consummation of the age. Amen (so let it be).

I declare to share the Good News to all and not be ashamed of Your Gospel according to Luke 4:16-19 So He came to Nazareth, [that Nazareth] where He had been brought up, and He entered the synagogue, as was His custom on the Sabbath day. And He stood up to read. And there was handed to Him [the roll of] the book of the prophet Isaiah. He opened (unrolled) the book and found the place where it was written, The Spirit of the Lord [is] upon Me, because He has anointed Me [the Anointed One, the Messiah] to preach the good news (the Gospel) to the poor; He has sent Me to announce release to the captives and recovery of sight to the blind, to send forth as delivered those who are oppressed [who are downtrodden, bruised, crushed, and broken down by calamity], To proclaim the acceptable year of the Lord [the day when salvation and the free favors of God profusely abound.

I declare to love one another and discern your body each and every part. I declare to obey your voice, Lord Jesus. I shall supernaturally prosper and be in health, and no evil shall ever overtake me. Your Church shall be multiplied in number and quality. Help me to visit the imprisoned and feed the hungry.

Father your church and I shall live in love, righteousness, abundance, joy, peace and your divine health and safety every minute, every day all year long. I commit myself to this time of consecration, fasting and prayer.

CHAPTER SEVEN

THE PLACE TO EXPERIENCE GOD'S GLORY

AND WHEN the day of Pentecost had fully come, they were all assembled together in one place, ²When suddenly there came a sound from heaven like the rushing of a violent tempest blast, and it filled the whole house in which they were sitting. ³And there appeared to them tongues resembling fire, which were separated and distributed and which settled on each one of them. ⁴And they were all filled (diffused throughout their souls) with the Holy Spirit and began to speak in other (different, foreign) languages (tongues), as the Spirit kept giving them clear and loud expression [in each tongue in appropriate words].
Acts 2:1-4 (Amplified Bible)

Isn't it wonderful to sense the awesome presence of God? We read in the bible that Moses, Isaiah, Jacob and many others had an experience with the awesome presence of God. If ever you are going to experience the glorious presence of God you must get to the Birthing Floor. The Birthing Floor is a place to experience God's Glory; it's a place of prayer and intercession. The bible both describe the Glory of God and how God can and will choose the forces of nature to convince mankind of His available Glory. In the Old Testament you can read that the children of Israel experience the Glory of God with a cloud by day and a pillar of fire by night. Those were demonstrations of Gods glory and it was used so that the children of Israel would stay very close to God and follow Him. As you enter in the birthing floor and experience the Glory of God, desire to be drawn closer to him and believe that God will conceive power and destiny inside of you.

If you study the life of the Children of Israel you will see that those who chose to stay close to the cloud of His anointing were never be left behind. When you draw near to God through prayer and follow his instruction you will never be left behind. The cloud was a compelling force of nature for the Godly people. But for those who did not recognize it as being the Lord, they called it strange phenomena. They were impressed, but they were not compelled to follow Him! Today the Glory of God is a compelling force of the anointing for you. If you are unable to recognize the anointing as being the Glory of God and what the Lord is doing in your life then you will miss God's perfect timing for your life. Some people in Moses' days became disheartened, easily discouraged, or even complacent with what God was doing. Some were frightened by the glory of God and refused to follow what they did not understand. As a result many of them were left behind and suffered in the wilderness.

Have you ever thought about what a cloud can do? It can become a fog, a mist, a shower, a heavy downpour, sleet, hail, snow, a tornado, a twister, a typhoon or a hurricane. These phenomenas of nature can put the fear of God in any weather man! The Weather Channel can't do anything about what God chooses to do with His clouds. God is God. There is none other. You may not understand the Glory of God any better than how a cloud works, but that won't change the way God chooses to demonstrate His Glory.

Just as in the Old and New Testament, there will be those who will choose not to follow the Glory of God. You may be just that person. The people of the Old Testament who saw the Glory of God were good people just like you. They went to their synagogues every Sabbath. But they did not keep up with what God was doing because they didn't agree or they didn't understand it. They were left behind. They missed what God had for them! God have something for you and that is the very thing you had been praying for over the years. But you must be very careful and don't ever miss God and what he is doing, or else you will miss what you have asked him for. Do you miss your blessing in the midst of ignorance. It is time that you change your mindset and get in position with God and experience his Glory in your life. Many good people have purposely chosen to not allow the Glory of God in their lives, refused to change and lost their destiny and fall out of alignment and lose their blessings, their purpose and even their ministry.

You need to understand that just as there are many ways that God will use a cloud, there are many ways that He will manifest or demonstrate His Glory! You need to know that God is omnipresent. He is universal in where He is at all times. When Isaiah saw the Lord in Isaiah chapter 6, he heard the seraphim say, "Holy, holy, holy is the LORD of hosts; the whole earth is full of His glory!" That tells me that the glory of God is on the mountain tops and He is down in the valleys. That is God just being God. He is everywhere.

The bible says in the book of 1 Corinthians 6:19 Do you not know that your body is the temple (the very sanctuary) of the Holy Spirit Who lives within you, Whom you have received [as a Gift] from God? You are not your own. Also you can read in 11 Corinthians 6:16-18 What agreement [can there be between] a temple of God and idols? For we are the temple of the living God; even as God said, I will dwell in and with and among them and will walk in and with and among them, and I will be their God, and they shall be My people. ¹⁷So, come out from among [unbelievers], and separate (sever) yourselves from them, says the Lord, and touch not [any] unclean thing; then I will receive you kindly and treat you with favor, ¹⁸And I will be a Father to you, and you shall be My sons and daughters, says the Lord Almighty.

While it is true that God is everywhere, there is a difference you need to consider. It is this: The manifestation of the Glory of God is to take place in His Temple and his temple is within you. In the book of II Chronicle chapter 5 we see the priests and the Levites finding the Glory of God in the Temple where they worshipped, it was their birthing floor. That Temple or birthing floor was built by a man named, Solomon. Things have changed with the Glory of God.

Solomon was right in what he said in chapter 6:2. "I have surely built You an exalted house, and a place for You to dwell in forever." So what is God saying, well he is saying that he has built you a new Temple. You are the exalted Temple of God. The manifestation of the Glory of God is to take place within your temple of God.

You have been chosen to contain the manifestation of the Glory of God. Isaiah 60:2 says, For behold, the darkness shall cover the earth, and deep darkness the people; but the LORD will arise over you, and His glory will be seen upon you. Likewise in John 2, we have the first miracle of Jesus when He turned the water into wine. This beginning of signs Jesus did in Cana of Galilee, and manifested His glory; The Glory of God was there at the wedding, but the manifestation took place in His miracles.

In the book of 1 Peter 4:12 the bible says Beloved, do not be amazed and bewildered at the fiery ordeal which is taking place to test your quality, as though something strange (unusual and alien to you and your position) were befalling you. [13]But insofar as you are sharing Christ's sufferings, rejoice, so that when His glory [full of radiance and splendor] is revealed, you may also rejoice with triumph [exultantly]. [14]If you are censured and suffer abuse [because you bear] the name of Christ, blessed [are you—happy, fortunate, to be envied, with life-joy, and satisfaction in God's favor and salvation, regardless of your outward condition], because the Spirit of glory, the Spirit of God, is resting upon you. On their part He is blasphemed, but on your part He is glorified. [15]But let none of you suffer as a murderer or a thief or any sort of criminal, or as a mischief-maker (a meddler) in the affairs of others [infringing on their rights]. [16]But if [one is ill-treated and suffers] as a Christian [which he is contemptuously called], let him not be ashamed, but give glory to God that he is [deemed worthy to suffer] in his name.

With all of this Truth, why do you keep waiting for the Glory of God to manifest in your life? Just remember it is God Who is waiting on you to release His Glory in you. You have the power to believe in yourself and call forth that release. If you believe then release yourself the Glory of God is waiting to manifest in you.

Probably you have been fasting and praying for a day, a week, a month and are disappointed when nothing happens. You cannot understand why you cannot sense the Glory of God. The time has come for the Glory of God to manifest itself in your "earthen vessels" at the birthing floor. Just believe in yourself and stay focus on the presence of God as you seek him at the birthing floor. And stop looking back, the problem is when you keep looking back at how the Glory of God used to be, you will miss out on how the Glory of God is and will be. This is much like the story of David and Goliath. Saul's armor was not what David needed. Things change for the people of God. What used to work when you were sixteen or the way the Glory of God used to manifest itself in you when you were twenty, may not be how it will manifest itself in you in the future. It is time that you experience the Glory of God and birth something new while you recognize God's glory.

The Glory of God operates in newness everyday. Old things are passed away. Behold all things are new. You cannot resist what the Glory of God is doing just because you may not understand everything that is going on. That can be one of your main hindrances.

The Glory of God manifested itself in a little boy (David) and he destroyed the biggest enemy they had ever seen. The Glory of God can lift you up and make you an overcomer in Christ, if you don't resist it. But if you resist it you will be defeated and left behind. Here you can find the problem why you were failing in most of the things you are doing. Don't choose to stick with how it used to be. The tradition of yesterday, stop refusing God and allow him to do something new in you. Stop doubting when you see things are not working out for you, stop saying "that can't be God...that is not the way it's done, this is nonsense I don't need this change" yes you need a change so that you can experience Gods Glory.

Always remember that the Glory of God is within you and you must allow it to have it's way in you. With the Glory of God, there will be changes in your life. His cloud will lead you where you have never been before. You must follow Him if you want God's Glory to manifest in your life. Do you want to experience his glory, well it's available to you, but first you must desire it and secondly get in position seek the face of God at the birthing floor. He goes to those who desire Him!

Look at Moses and how he desired Him and wanted God to show him his Glory. In the book of Exodus 24:15-18 the bible says Then Moses went up into the mountain, and the cloud covered the mountain. ¹⁶The glory of the Lord rested on Mount Sinai, and the cloud covered it for six days. On the seventh day [God] called to Moses out of the midst of the cloud. ¹⁷And the glory of the Lord appeared to the Israelites like devouring fire on the top of the mountain. ¹⁸Moses entered into the midst of the cloud and went up the mountain, and Moses was on the mountain forty days and nights.

In Exodus 34:29-30 the bible says And it came to pass, when Moses came down from mount Sinai with the two tables of testimony in Moses' hand, when he came down from the mount, that Moses wist not that the skin of his face shone while he talked with him. And when Aaron and all the children of Israel saw Moses, behold, the skin of his face shone; and they were afraid to come nigh him.

In Exodus 34:33-35 the bible says And [till] Moses had done speaking with them, he put a veil on his face. But when Moses went in before the LORD to speak with him, he took the veil off, until he came out. And he came out, and spake unto the children of Israel [that] which he was commanded. And the children of Israel saw the face of Moses, that the skin of Moses' face shone: and Moses put the veil upon his face again, until he went in to speak with him.

When Moses went into the presence of God He heard the word of God speaking to him. Moses was given instruction concerning the Tabernacle of God. Moses was given details about the Tabernacle. God showed him the pattern of it. When you enter the birthing floor, seek him and spend time with God he will show you how to bring your dreams and vision into reality. Again you must know that unless God builds for you, you will build in vain. If you get in position to seek him, his Glory will show up. God's glory appeared to Moses as devouring fire. And the light that shone from the fire of God actually was absorbed into Moses face and he shone with the same light that He saw.

When he came down from the mountain to give Israel the words of God, he did not know it, but his face was shining bright with a glow. This was not a happy expression on his face that people saw, as though we say today, "Doesn't he have a glow on his face," referring to his happiness. This was literal light. If Moses walked into a dark cave, he would have lit the cave up with the light from his face. Moses did not know He shone like that. And the people did not want to look at it, so Moses put a veil on his face. Imagine Moses standing before you with a veil on his face, so you could not see one part of his face as he preached to you.

When God's word comes to you, it is said in the Bible that light comes to you. And many times some people see that light and others do not. Others are veil from it. In Hebrews 10:20 we read a statement that tells us that a veil, in the Bible, represents human flesh. Hebrews said "By a new and living way, which he hath consecrated for us, through the veil, that is to say, his flesh;"

Now, when the Bible refers to the flesh and walking after the flesh, for example, it refers to the material things and material concerns of a person that take up all that person's attention. Fleshly people are people who are materialistic-minded. They are very physical-minded people. The things that your flesh is concerned with would be physical things in life, such as work, what clothes we wear, what events happened with your friends... anything that is not spiritual is fleshly.

Fleshly things are not always bad. Some people think that being carnal means one is evil. But carnal only means fleshly. Yes, there are some carnal things that are bad. But there are some good carnal things. Marriage, cars, money, jobs, friends are all carnal things. Carnal things are fine if they are in their proper priority. But when it comes to the Word of God and hearing God speak to you, you need to get your hearts involved and open your spirits up to God. You do not need your hearts in your jobs. You do not use your spirits when you are figuring out what you need for groceries this week, or what bills are due this week. And you can get by in everything in the world without using your spirits and the part of yourself that is spiritual.

But one place where your spirits mean everything and your hearts are most important is when you come to hear the word of the living God. There is a part of you that is spiritual. God is a Spirit.

And every human has a spirit. Most people do not even know it exists. They know a lot about emotions and intelligence, things of the soul, but not very much at all about the things of the spirit. And some people who try to understand the spirit believe there are such things as ghosts and horoscopes that tell your fortune and are completely out in left field with crazy ideas. But you need to have no veil of fleshliness over your heart when you hear the Word of God.

Moses saw somewhat of God's glory with open face. When God spoke to him, Moses' mind was on nothing else. But when he came down to give the same word to the people, and his face shone with the glory that he saw, the people wanted a veil over his face. And Paul said this about them in 2 Corinthians Nor [do we act] like Moses, who put a veil over his face so that the Israelites might not gaze upon the finish of the vanishing [splendor which had been upon it].

They could not look at the end of what he said. End, in such context in the Bible, means Purpose. They did not see the Purpose of what he said. When you receive the LIGHT of the Word of God, you will shine yourself. But if you are veiled from it by fleshliness, you will not shine and you will not comprehend the Word spoken to you. You could have comprehended it, but you chose to think on fleshly things instead. That is why the Bible says: IN THE beginning [before all time] was the Word (Christ), and the Word was with God, and the Word was God Himself. ²He was present originally with God. ³All things were made and came into existence through Him; and without Him was not even one thing made that has come into being. ⁴In Him was Life, and the Life was the Light of men. ⁵And the Light shines on in the darkness, for the darkness has never overpowered it [put it out or absorbed it or appropriated it, and is unreceptive to it].

You remain in darkness when you do not comprehend the light. Everyone in the world who is not shining in God's Glory is a person who never did comprehend the word of God. They may not have heard it yet, or they heard it, but a veil of Fleshly thinking blocked their minds from the light. But on the other hand, if you comprehend the word when it is preached to you, you begin to absorb that light and you start to shine yourself. This is not a physical light we are talking about, as it was physical in Moses' face. But this is a far deeper glory, it's completely Spiritual.

There are people who say they are Christians and never actually absorb any light from the Word. Paul told them to arise and Christ would give them light. Notice that Moses went up into the mountain and saw light of God's glory. And when he came down, he shone with the same light. You must arise get down on your knees position yourself at the birthing floor.

Isaiah 2:2-3 says And it shall come to pass in the last days, [that] the mountain of the LORD'S house shall be established in the top of the mountains, and shall be exalted above the hills; and all nations shall flow unto it. And many people shall go and say, Come ye, and let us go up to the mountain of the LORD, to the house of the God of Jacob; and he will teach us of his ways, and we will walk in his paths: for out of Zion shall go forth the law, and the word of the LORD from Jerusalem.

Mica 4:1-2 says But in the last days it shall come to pass, [that] the mountain of the house of the LORD shall be established in the top of the mountains, and it shall be exalted above the hills; and people shall flow unto it. And many nations shall come, and say, Come, and let us go up to the mountain of the LORD, and to the house of the God of Jacob; and he will teach us of his ways, and we will walk in his paths: for the law shall go forth of Zion, and the word of the LORD from Jerusalem.

When you get to the birthing floor God will take you up upon a mountain to show you how to bring those things you are carrying within you into reality. John went up upon a mountain and was shown the New Jerusalem. Revelation 21:10 And he carried me away in the spirit to a great and high mountain, and shewed me that great city, the holy Jerusalem, descending out of heaven from God,

God took John higher than a mountain, and took him into heaven in Revelation four and was shown things. Revelation 4:1 After this I looked, and, behold, a door [was] opened in heaven: and the first voice which I heard [was] as it were of a trumpet talking with me; which said, Come up hither, and I will shew thee things which must be hereafter.

By the time you finish reading this book I trust that you will be able to say, "I've been on the mountain with Jesus." Jesus took James, John and Peter on a mountain in Matthew 17, and they saw him change and shine like the sun. They saw His glory. His true identity, so to speak. Come up to the mountain top with me and see His glory!!

Look at Isaiah 60:1-5 the bible says ARISE [from the depression and prostration in which circumstances have kept you—rise to a new life]! Shine (be radiant with the glory of the Lord), for your light has come, and the glory of the Lord has risen upon you! ²For behold, darkness shall cover the earth, and dense darkness [all] peoples, but the Lord shall arise upon you [O Jerusalem], and His glory shall be seen on you. ³And nations shall come to your light, and kings to the brightness of your rising ⁴Lift up your eyes round about you and see! They all gather themselves together, they come to you. Your sons shall come from afar, and your daughters shall be carried and nursed in the arms. ⁵Then you shall see and be radiant, and your heart shall thrill and tremble with joy [at the glorious deliverance] and be enlarged; because the abundant wealth of the [Dead] Sea shall be turned to you, unto you shall the nations come with their treasures.

When Isaiah wrote, arise and shine, the Hebrew word for shine also means be enlightened. When you enliven something, you give it life and it lives. When you enlighten something, you give it light and it shines. You are changed. Let the Glory of God shine upon you and you need to soak it up and when you walk the devil will see that you are shining with spiritual glory from God's Word. Moses' face shone after God spoke to him about the tabernacle. God's Word is about His tabernacle. His tabernacle in the Old Testament was a tent that he allowed Israel to build wherein his Spirit actually manifested. It manifested, or actually was sensed by the five senses. Gods Tabernacle today is you and when he begins to talk to you it meant that he wants you to know that he is about to dwell in you because you are a temple of the Holy Spirit, and you need to comprehend that, and receive it, and put your whole attention to this very important desire of God, then something will shine in you and bring you forth into destiny.

The bible says in 1 John 1:5 This then is the message which we have heard of him, and declare unto you, that God is light, and in him is no darkness at all.

If God is light and he talks to us about how he wants a tabernacle, and we are his tabernacle, well it only stands to reason that he wants his light inside of us, his spirit, and we will SHINE with HIS GLORY! Notice what Paul said about this veil and Moses:

2 Corinthians 3:12-13 Seeing then that we have such hope, we use great plainness of speech: {plainness: or, boldness} And not as Moses, [which] put a veil over his face, that the children of Israel could not stedfastly look to the end of that which is abolished:

Come to the birthing floor a place of meeting with God and experience his glory and when you come you will meet with Jesus. Get away from all the outward things of the world, your jobs, your situations at the bank, your situations with the family, and rise up to spiritual higher things. And as you go to the birthing floor to meet with God remove all veiling from your hearts. Empty your minds of all the things of the flesh and physical and get ready to comprehend some spiritual things.

When you enter into the birthing floor which is your prayer closet purpose in your heart to get out of the things of the flesh for a while and open our spirits to God. Get that argument you and your friend had out of your mind, because that will only veil you away from the spiritual things you are seeking after. Get your mind off everything that will hinder you from experiencing God's Glory in your life.

It is time that God raised you above all principalities and powers and made you sit together with him in heavenly places, so that you can go out and let the devil know he can't beat you down over how "no-good" you were. The only reason the devil can condemn you with his lies is when you already look down upon yourself. If you know what the Word said about you, and you know that you are Holy and Sanctified in Christ Jesus, then when the devil comes in to condemn you, you would just have to laugh in his face! But there are times when Satan succeeds over you and the reason he is successful at condemning you is because you fail to comprehended who you have in you and that is Christ. So know who you are in

Christ Jesus. Just remember God has removed all the past of those who repented and were baptized, and you are shining.

Don't you ever allow Satan to condemned you and remind you of your past when in actuality God sees nothing but a person in his son whose condemnable past was buried and is no longer a part of you. It is time that you start to focus on the positive. When you focus on the positive the positive will get bigger in you and when you focus on the negative the negative will get bigger in you. So focus on the positive things in life.

The bible says in 2 Corinthians 5:14-17 For the love of Christ constraineth us; because we thus judge, that if one died for all, then were all dead: And [that] he died for all, that they which live should not henceforth live unto themselves, but unto him which died for them, and rose again. Wherefore henceforth know we no man after the flesh: yea, though we have known Christ after the flesh, yet now henceforth know we [him] no more. Wherefore if any man [be] in Christ, [he is] a new creature: old things are passed away; behold, all things are become new.

Just remember your old things are passed away, it is dead and gone. The bible says if any man be in Christ he is a new creature. So stop thinking about what had happened in the past. If you think, "No not me. I am no-good." Well that is foolishness! The bible says any man is a new creature when he/she is in CHRIST. The bible says in 2 Corinthians 5:21 For he hath made him [to be] sin for us, who knew no sin; that we might be made the righteousness of God in him.

Hear what God thinks of us? You are the righteousness of God. So why are you still feeling condemnation. Just believe what God says and believe how God sees you. Renew your mind to the way God thinks of you. He looks at you as in his son Jesus.

CHAPTER EIGHT

THE BIRTHING OF BREAKTHORUGH

The Lord is close to those who are of a broken heart and saves such as are crushed with sorrow for sin and are humbly and thoroughly penitent. Psalm 34:18 (Amplified Bible)

[17]My sacrifice [the sacrifice acceptable] to God is a broken spirit; a broken and a contrite heart [broken down with sorrow for sin and humbly and thoroughly penitent], such, O God, You will not despise. Psalm 51:17 (Amplified Bible)

What is it that you want God to do for you and will it require a spiritual and emotional breakthrough in order for it to come to pass in your life? Do you have the faith to trust God to take the steps He is going to lay out for you when you seek His face at the birthing floor and get the necessary information through His word and through wise instruction from those who have been there? In order for your breakthrough to come to pass it will require you to see your situation with different eyes, a different and fresh perspective. Sometimes to gain that new perspective, you not only need to give the situation time in prayer, but you also need to break the strongholds of emotion through prevailing prayer and fasting. Your brokenness can bring your breakthrough.

Brokenness can bring you to a new dimension in God through which no other doors may lead. There are places God wants to bring you, but the price of admission is brokenness. You can't get to these places through faith, through victory or through praise; it will take just your brokenness.

Now although not a bone of our Lord was broken, when the Lord was crucified and bore our sins in His body, the Bible describes His body as being broken: 1 Corinthians 11:24 says And when He had given thanks, He broke [it] and said, Take, eat. This is My body, which is broken for you. Do this to call Me [affectionately] to remembrance.

Jesus Christ was broken, but through His brokenness, salvation was made available for you, but salvation cannot be known without repentance and a place of brokenness is necessary for repentance, the Bible says Godly sorrow worketh repentance. We must be broken before we can be fixed!

In each of our lives, God had designed a process of growth and development. And brokenness symbolizes humility before God. It symbolizes total surrender to His work and His will, after all, God can't resist brokenness. He is, in fact attracted to your brokenness, it draws Him to us.

When the broken and repentant heart is confessing their sins before God and is turning from the wrong, He will pay attention! He just can't resist humility and brokenness! One thing that will actually happen when you enter into the birthing floor brokenness and humility will just fall into place. That is what prayer and a heart of willingness will do to you.

James 4:6-10 says But He gives us more and more grace (power of the Holy Spirit, to meet this evil tendency and all others fully). That is why He says, God sets Himself against the proud and haughty, but gives grace [continually] to the lowly (those who are humble enough to receive it).

[7]So be subject to God. Resist the devil [stand firm against him], and he will flee from you.

⁸Come close to God and He will come close to you. [Recognize that you are] sinners, get your soiled hands clean; [realize that you have been disloyal] wavering individuals with divided interests, and purify your hearts [of your spiritual adultery].

⁹[As you draw near to God] be deeply penitent and grieve, even weep [over your disloyalty]. Let your laughter be turned to grief and your mirth to dejection and heartfelt shame [for your sins].

¹⁰Humble yourselves [feeling very insignificant] in the presence of the Lord, and He will exalt you [He will lift you up and make your lives significant].

Now this is opposite of your thinking, this speaks of getting down to be lifted up. Well you may say that this doesn't make any sense but try to go higher and higher and not lower and see what will or can happen to you. The lower you go and step into humility the more you can trust God and bring you into your breakthrough. Because God is saying in the midst of brokenness you will experience your breakthrough because brokenness brings breakthrough. What God wants you to know is that he is trying to tell you to stop and try to lean not on your own understanding but his and he will direct you to your breakthrough.

God wants you to let go of your personal desires and trust him for his provision, He is willing to do great things through you and all he is waiting for is that you get yourself out of his way so that he can give you your breakthrough.

There is a clear pattern in the Bible that teaches us that Brokenness Brings Breakthrough. Before Abraham became the father of many nations, he and Sarah were childless. Before Jacob could be blessed, he was wounded by angel in a wrestling match. Before Joseph ruled Egypt, he was thrown into a pit, sold into slavery, and falsely imprisoned. Before Job's estate was doubled, he lost everything he had, including his family, his fortune, and his future. Before Moses became the great deliverer, he lost his position, his possessions, and his popularity. Before Joshua conquered the Promised Land, he went through the wilderness.

Before Samson crushed the Philistines, he was blinded, binded, and grinded. Before David became king, he was renounced by his family, ridiculed by his foes, and rejected by his friends. Before Daniel could be used mightily, he had to spend the night in the lion's den. Before Hosea became a powerful spokesman for God, his wife betrayed him, which broke him. Before Peter preached 3,000 souls into the kingdom, he denied his Savior three times and went out and wept bitterly. Before Paul brought the gospel to the Gentiles, he was blinded on the Damascus road.

There are times when God has to break you so that He can remake you to his likeness. The bible says in Jeremiah 18:4 And the vessel that he made of clay was marred in the hand of the potter: so he made it again another vessel, as seemed good to the potter to make it. Also Psalm 51:8 says Make me to hear joy and gladness; that the bones which thou hast broken may rejoice.

The songwriter expressed the proper attitude we should have during the times when we are broken: *Have Thine own way, Lord. Have Thine own way. Thou art the Potter, I am the clay. Mold me and make me. After thy will. While I am waiting, Yielded and still.*

The Potter is able to mend the broken vessel and use it for His own purposes and pleasure! But if you never find a place of brokenness and submission to His will in your lives, you will never know breakthrough. If you are not broken, then you cannot be made into the image He has designed for you. Brokenness will cause you to welcome the unique talents, gifts and ministries that God has granted you.

Well you may ask what good can come out of me after all this brokenness. The same question was asked by Nathanael in the New Testament. "Can Any Good Thing Come Out of Nazareth"

The bible says in Genesis 49:13 Zebulun shall dwell at the haven of the sea; and he shall be for an haven of ships; and his border shall be unto Zidon. Also John 1:46 says And Nathanael said unto him, Can there any good thing come .out of Nazareth? Philip saith unto him, Come and see.

Have you ever wished you lived in another place after all you have been through or are going through? I believe on occasion, most of us have entertained that thought. Not only have we wished we could live in another city, but some have even wished they could have been born in another class or race.

In many instances, It appears that those who are successful in life seem to have prestigious histories that have begun in some far away places removed from their rural existence or poor inner city neighborhoods. We have to dispell the myth that a person must be from "somewhere else" to make a significant contribution to the Kingdom of God. The place where anyone is from is somewhere else, to someone else!

One of the frustrations you personally may have is feelings that life would have been better if circumstances would have been different. Asking yourself these questions: Why wasn't I born to a rich family? Why couldn't I have the physical appearance of others? Why can't I do as well in my studies as others?

Probably you have even ponder the thought that life would be better for you if you had different parents and a different home. You have created a virtual fantasy world in which you attempt to appear more than you actually are. You invent experiences you have not known, and generally live a fabricated existence.

I know that your experiences in life may slow you down. And start your race with a more difficult course ahead of you. It doesn't mean that you can't win, but it does mean that you must have a tremendous amount of discipline and will power to achieve your goals and have a breakthrough. Even more than the person who runs the inside lane. That's where God comes in the picture. Whether you are running the inside track or the outside lane, whether you are born into poverty or to a life of relative comfort, the greatest achievement comes to those who put God first. Probably you know someone who achieved some level of success without God, but those who let him control their lives have gone even higher than they could have imagined.

As a believer in Christ, you have to come to know that God is able to lift you from obscurity to the pinnacles of success, if you will allow him to work through you to benefit his kingdom. Whether you were born in a mansion or a shack, there is no limit to what a child of God can do or where he or she can go. It's all in God's hand.

Actually we see in the bible focuses on Nathaniel's question, "Can any good thing come out of Nazareth? The greatest understanding of the text comes from realizing that it is rooted in a history that began with Jacob in the Old Testament. Jacob had twelve sons: Levi, Simeon, Judah, Joseph, Issachar, Dan, Benjamin, Asher, Gad, Naphtali, Rueben, and Zebulun. These twelve sons all received an inheritance from Jacob who also added blessings to some of them.

Among the least of the inheritances is that given to Zebulun. Zebulun, remember him? He was the sixth and last child of Leah, whom Jacob was forced to marry after working seven years for her younger sister Rachel. He was told that his descendants would be those who would dwell by the sea, at the very edge of land of promise. Hundreds of years later as the Children of Israel overcame slavery and marched into the Promised Land, the 12 tribes divided up the new land.

In keeping with the blessings of Jacob, the tribe of Zebulun was given an area of land that was near the sea of Galilee. It appeared to be a very mediocre inheritance. While his brothers received inheritances that included mountains, fertile fields and pasture land that could support sheep and cattle, all Zebulun received was an address, a small area of land next to the sea that would not be able to grow anything or produce much profit. His brothers appeared the more prosperous. His family appeared the losers.

The land that Zebulun came to inherit was one of the most despised places among the people of God. His land was way in the north, way at the very top; his land was bordering the sea on one side, and Sidon of the Gentiles on the other side, it was a long way from Jerusalem where the king would come to live lives, where the leaders would come to reside. His land is far removed; perhaps once a year he would go there.

The historian Josephus notes that Zebulun's lands reached on the one side to the Lake of Gennesareth and on the other to Carmel and the Mediterranean. On the south it was bounded by Issachar, whose inheritance lay in the great plain or valley of the Kishon; on the north it had Naphtali and Asher. Thus, it was remote from the center of government.

By any standard Zebulun was so far North that it rarely participated in tribal decisions, central government or other activities. For the most part, it was what we would consider "backwoods " or a "one red light" town. Morever, it was assumed that those who came from Galilee or any of the cities of that area, they were generally considered what we would call "hicks" "unlearned", "uncultured" with little or no chance of achieving success.. At the least, those who were descendants of Zebulun were disappointed. What they had was very small. It was nothing to speak of, but it was theirs. It had been given to them by God himself.

The descendants of Zebulun took their small inheritance by the sea and turned it into a prosperous way of life, which profited from the sea. They became industrious in many ways that used the resources that were available to them. Although despised by the rest of the nation, they silently worked to being a successful existence for themselves, even while everyone else laughed.

Zebulun worked against the odds. The chances of succeeding in such a remote area were very low. Very few doubted that the tribe would even continue to exist let alone thrive. Yet Zebulunites used what was around them and succeeded anyway.

Are you facing similar situations and are operating in very difficult situations. Do you feel abused and misused. Well they felt discarded and trampled upon so much that they felt like doormats. It's difficult to think of yourself in any way but a failure when everyone seems to think you are a Zebulunite or a good for nothing! Zebulunites, however, are overcomers! They achieved despite the odds! They excelled despite their detractors! They made it to the top despite their critics!

Every Zebulunite needs discipline. This is the ability to force oneself to do what is necessary to overcome. It may mean forcing yourself to achieve. Secondly every Zebulunite needs wisdom. Wisdom goes beyond mere knowledge. It is the wise application of knowledge. Someone said wisdom is knowing, "When to say yes, When to say no, when to hold on and when to let go!"

What Zebulunite can ever hope to achieve anything without determination? Determination is the unquenchable fire that fuels the quest for success. It is that inner push that resolves to go forward despite obstacles. If you put a Zebulunite in a boat that is sinking, he will keep searching until he finds a way to plug the hole and bailout the water or swim for the shore. He won't sit still and drown! So you need to know that if you go forth out of your Nazareth you must remember one truth, when God blesses, it doesn't matter where you live, or the extent of your circumstance, he's able to see it through so that you can experience your breakthrough.

The Zubulunites didn't have much, but what little they had was blessed by God. When what you have has been blessed by God, it doesn't matter who you are or where you are from, the power of God makes the difference! All Moses had was a rod, but when it was blessed by God it turned water to blood and opened up the Red Sea! All Elijah had was a mantle on his shoulders, but when it was blessed by God it performed hundreds of miracles!. All a widow woman had was an empty barrel, but when it was blessed by God, that barrel never ran dry. All the lame man had were two legs that would not walk, but when blessed by God those legs were able to walk!

When Philip came to Nathaniel he said "come see the savior." Immediately Nathaniel wanted to know, where is he from? Did he come from Jericho, known for its high and lofty walled cities? Did he come from Bethlehem, riddled with many taverns and inns? Did he come from Emmaus, along whose road many great men have walked and talked? Did he come from Bethany, in whose gardens many pious and devout men have prayed? Did he come from Jerusalem, whose temple echoes the voice of God?

When Philip responded that he was from Nazareth, the question responded, "Can any good thing come out of Nazareth? Philip could only answer come and see! Come and see and I'll show you a man out of Nazareth, who is making the lame walk again!

CHAPTER NINE

BREAKING FORTH TO BIRTH THE NEW ME

Come to Me, all you who labor and are heavy-laden and overburdened, and I will cause you to rest. [I will ease and relieve and refresh]your souls.] 29 Take My yoke upon you and learn of Me, for I am gentle (meek) and humble (lowly) in heart, and you will find rest (relief and ease and refreshment and recreation and blessed quiet) for your souls. 30 For My yoke is wholesome (useful, good—not harsh, hard, sharp, or pressing, but comfortable, gracious, and pleasant), and My burden is light and easy to be borne.
Matthew 11:28-30 (Amplified Bible)

God's desire is to bring you to an expected end: The bible says in Jeremiah 29:11 For I know the thoughts and plans that I have for you, says the Lord, thoughts and plans for welfare and peace and not for evil, to give you hope in your final outcome. That expected end is fulfillment of the vision for yourself and finishing the work of God:

Jesus said My meat is to do the will of Him that sent me, and to finish His work, according to John 4:34 whenever you enter into something new, it always requires leaving the old. Birth requires leaving the security of the womb. God is asking you to take a new step of faith: According to the Living Bible in Isaiah 43:18 it says But the Lord says, Do not cling to events of the past or dwell on what happened long ago. Watch for the new thing I am going to do. It is happening already you can see it now.

You may have been bound by doctrine which claims the power of God is no longer for today. You may have thought the extension of the Gospel to the world was the responsibility of ministers or missionaries. You may have been bound by tradition or denominations which prevented you from joining hands with the rest of the Body of Christ in the harvest fields of the Lord. But God has given you a new vision. You are becoming part of a new network of spiritual laborers bound together by unity of purpose.

The Bible records two separate incidents involving the use of a net in the natural world which illustrate a great spiritual truth. The first event occurred at the beginning of Christ's earthly ministry and is recorded in Luke 5. The disciples had been fishing all night and caught nothing. Jesus told them: Launch out into the deep and let down your nets for a draught according to Luke 5:4 But Peter said: Master, we have toiled all the night and have taken nothing; nevertheless at thy word I will let down the net according to Luke 5:5.

When they let down the net they caught so many fish that it broke and they had to call their partners in another boat to come help them. The catch was so great that it filled both boats and they began to sink. Peter was amazed at this but Jesus told him: Fear not, from henceforth thou shalt catch men according to Luke 5:10. The catch Peter was experiencing in the natural world was nothing compared to the great harvest he would reap in the spirit world as he became a fisher of men. A similar incident is recorded at the end of Christ's ministry in John 21. The disciples had fished all night and caught nothing. At Christ's command they cast in the net and, once again, it was filled with fish. But this time was different than the first. The net did not break: Simon Peter went up and drew the net to land full of great fishes, an hundred and fifty and three; and for all there were so many, yet was not the net broken according to John 21:11

These two events actually happened in the natural world, but they were parallels of a great spiritual truth. The first time the net broke but the second time it did not. What made the difference?

The first net was an example of the efforts of man. Peter was a fisherman by trade. He knew the natural methods and the tradition of fishermen. Through the broken net Jesus showed him that the efforts of man could not fulfill the vision and work of God. When Peter realized the great work to which God was calling him he cried out: Depart from me; for I am a sinful man, O Lord, according to Luke 5:8

Peter would become a fisher of men. The old network could not accommodate the great spiritual harvest. Peter would have to abandon the traditions of man. He must cross the line of separation between Jew and Gentile. The old network must be broken and he must become part of a new network. When you find yourself with God he will bring people who will help you to maintain your walk with him and help you to fulfill your vision.

Jesus did not come to destroy the old, but to fulfill it through the new. He did not destroy the law, but added new meaning to it. He did not abolish the blood sacrifice for sin, but fulfilled it through the shedding of His own blood for the remission of sin. Jesus warned about putting new wine into old wineskins. The old wineskins would not be able to hold the new wine just as the net could not hold the fish. The challenge of the Great Commission cannot be accomplished with anything less than a new net in the spirit world. Between the first and the second fishing trips, a new network had been created. These natural fishing incidents were parallels of what had happened in the spirit world.

This new spiritual network can accommodate the vision which Jesus gave. But to enter it, one must step from the old into the new. The old yoke must be broken. The old net must be destroyed in order for the new net to hold.

Yokes were used all over the ancient world to unite animals together to labor in the harvest fields. They are still used for this purpose in many nations today. Jesus spoke of the yoke when He said in Matthew 11:28-30 Come to Me, all you who labor and are heavy-laden and overburdened, and I will cause you to rest. [I will ease and relieve and refresh your souls.]

29Take My yoke upon you and learn of Me, for I am gentle (meek) and humble (lowly) in heart, and you will find rest (relief and ease and refreshment and recreation and blessed quiet) for your souls. 30 For My yoke is wholesome (useful, good—not harsh, hard, sharp, or pressing, but comfortable, gracious, and pleasant), and My burden is light and easy to be borne.

This vision He has given is not for your personal gain only but also for the harvest field. Today that field represents three billion people who have never received the Gospel message. And He tells us this challenge is "easy" and "light"?

That is exactly what He is saying. But the old network, the old yoke, cannot accommodate the vision. You cannot fulfill it in yourself. You cannot do it through the efforts of man. You must become part of the new network and be yoked together with Him.

We are all under a yoke of some type. You are either under the yoke of bondage or you are under the yoke of God. The yoke of bondage is three-fold. You can be in bondage to either sin, self, or man. God said I am the Lord your God, which brought you forth out of the land of Egypt [sin] that ye should not be their bondmen; and I have broken the bands of your yoke, and made you go upright according to Leviticus 26:13 The yoke of Egypt means the yoke of sin. You must have the yoke of sin broken in your lives if you are to come under the yoke with Jesus.

The yoke of bondage can be a bondage to self: Romans 7:15 says For that which I do I allow not; for what I would, that I do not; but what I hate, that do I. Selfishness and pride are examples of the yoke of self. The yoke of man is bondage put on you by others: Matthews 23:4 For they bind heavy burdens and grievous to be borne and lay them on men's shoulders but they themselves will not move them with one of their fingers. The yoke of man can include the bondage of guilt, tradition, denomination, or impossible standards of behavior imposed by others. The three-fold yoke of bondage of sin, self, and man speaks of imposed labor, heaviness, and restlessness.

The yoke of God speaks of a united labor instead of imposed labor. It speaks of lightness instead of heaviness. It is a yoke of rest instead of restlessness. The three-fold yoke of God is easy, light and restful: Jesus said in Matthew 11:28-30 Come unto Me, all ye that labour and are heavy laden, and I will give you rest. Take My yoke upon you, and learn of Me; for I am meek and lowly in heart: and ye shall find rest unto your souls. For My yoke is easy, and My burden is light. There are three steps to bridge the gap. Jesus provided three steps to bridge the gap between the yoke of bondage and the yoke of God. It is the way out of the old into the new:

Come: You must willingly come to Him. This destroys the yoke of sin.

Take: You must take His yoke. In doing so, the yoke of man is destroyed.

Learn: By learning of Him you destroy the yoke of self.

The yoke of God is not simply imparted by Him. It is shared by Him. It is God's desire that every yoke of sin, self, and man in your life be broken. It is necessary if you are to fulfill the vision. In one Old Testament record, Israel was surrounded by the enemy (army of the Assyrians.)

God spoke to Israel and declared: Isaiah 14:24-26 says The Lord of hosts has sworn, saying, Surely, as I have thought and planned, so shall it come to pass, and as I have purposed, so shall it stand 25 That I will break the Assyrian in My land, and upon My mountains I will tread him underfoot. Then shall the [Assyrian's] yoke depart from [the people of Judah], and his burden depart from their shoulders. This is the [Lord's] purpose that is purposed upon the whole earth [regarded as conquered and put under tribute by Assyria]; and this is [His omnipotent] hand that is stretched out over all the nations.

You can also see in verse 26 that God wanted to break the yoke from off the neck of Israel. But His purpose extended beyond Israel to the nations of the world: What was God's purpose? His purpose was that the yoke of bondage be broken from the nations of the world. A few chapters later it is recorded that: The angel of the Lord went forth and smote in the camp of the Assyrians a hundred and fourscore and five thousand: and when they arose early in the morning, behold they were all dead corpses according to Isaiah 37:36 God wants every yoke in your life to become as a dead corpse. He wants to destroy it in order to bring you under the yoke with Him.

How will this yoke be broken well Isaiah 10:27 says "and the yoke shall be destroyed because of the anointing." It will not be destroyed by deep teaching. It will not be destroyed by psychology or education. -It will not be destroyed through counseling or through an organization or denomination. It will be destroyed by the anointing of the Holy Spirit which is the power of God. But God's purpose for breaking the yoke extends beyond your life to the nations of the world. He wants to break the yoke of bondage in your life to enable you to fulfill the vision of breaking the yoke from the nations of the world:

This is the purpose that is purposed upon the whole earth: And this is the hand that is stretched out upon all the nations. For the Lord of hosts hath purposed, and who shall disannul it? And His hand is stretched out, and who shall turn it back? According to Isaiah 14:26-27 God said: Is not this the fast that I have chosen? to loose the bands of wickedness, to undo the heavy burdens and to let the oppressed go free and that ye break every yoke? According to Isaiah 58:6 Then He listed the results of breaking the yoke:

Then you shall call, and the Lord will answer; you shall cry, and He will say, Here I am. If you take away from your midst yokes of oppression [wherever you find them], the finger pointed in scorn [toward the oppressed or the godly], and every form of false, harsh, unjust, and wicked speaking,

10And if you pour out that with which you sustain your own life for the hungry and satisfy the need of the afflicted, then shall your light rise in darkness, and your obscurity and gloom become like the noonday.

11And the Lord shall guide you continually and satisfy you in drought and in dry places and make strong your bones. And you shall be like a watered garden and like a spring of water whose waters fail not.

12And your ancient ruins shall be rebuilt; you shall raise up the foundations of [buildings that have laid waste for] many generations; and you shall be called Repairer of the Breach, Restorer of Streets to Dwell In according to Isaiah 58:9-12.

The results of the breaking of the yoke of bondage are: You will know the voice of God. You will call, and the Lord will answer, "Here I am." You will be successful in the fulfillment of your vision. Your light will rise in obscurity which speaks of success.

The Lord will guide you continually. He will be your provision. You will be reproductive. You will be like a watered garden which is fruitful. You will be reproductive and those you produce in the spirit world will be reproductive. They will rise up to rebuild the old structures on the right foundation.

God promised Israel in the natural world: And the tree of the field shall yield her fruit, and the earth shall yield her increase, and they shall be safe in their land, and shall know that I am the Lord, when I have broken the bands of their yoke according to Ezekiel 34:27 The same is true in the spirit world. The breaking of the yoke results in spiritual productivity. The old network is inadequate, broken, and empty. It cannot accommodate the abundant harvest. The old yokes of tradition, denomination, self-effort, and unconcern must be broken. New foundations, new yokes, a new network are necessary to enter the gap between sinful man and a righteous God. The vision will only be fulfilled if you have experienced the anointing which breaks the yoke.

CHAPTER TEN

BIRTHING FREEDOM – DECLARATION

*So if the Son liberates you [makes you free men],
then you are really and unquestionably free.
John 8:36 (Amplified Bible)*

Now that you fully understand you purpose in God make the following declaration and let the devil know you are therefore now a new creature in Christ, the old has gone and the new has arrived.

My declaration according to Genesis 12:1-3, 7:

<u>God will reveal my spiritual destiny.</u>

¹NOW [in Haran] the Lord said to Abram, Go for yourself [for your own advantage] away from your country, from your relatives and your father's house, to the land that I will show you.

⁷Then the Lord appeared to Abram and said, I will give this land to your posterity. So Abram built an altar there to the Lord, Who had appeared to him.

<u>God will make my spiritual descendants great and he will bless me. He will make my name great-of good reputation. He will make me a blessing.</u>

²And I will make of you a great nation, and I will bless you [with abundant increase of favors] and make your name famous and distinguished, and you will be a blessing [dispensing good to others].

He will bless those that bless me and curse them that curse me. The families (nations) of the earth will be blessed through me.

³And I will bless those who bless you [who confer prosperity or happiness upon you] and curse him who curses or uses insolent language toward you; in you will all the families and kindred of the earth be blessed [and by you they will bless themselves].

My declaration according to Genesis 13:15-17:

All God reveals to me is mine. These blessings will extend to my spiritual seed.

¹⁵For all the land which you see I will give to you and to your posterity forever.

My spiritual seed will be as the dust of the earth.

¹⁶And I will make your descendants like the dust of the earth, so that if a man could count the dust of the earth, then could your descendants also be counted.

Wherever God leads me, that spiritual territory is mine.

¹⁷Arise, walk through the land, the length of it and the breadth of it, for I will give it to you.

My declaration according to Genesis 15:1-21:

God is my shield. God is my exceeding great reward.

¹AFTER THESE things, the word of the Lord came to Abram in a vision, saying, Fear not, Abram, I am your Shield, your abundant compensation, and your reward shall be exceedingly great.

I will bring forth spiritual heirs.

⁴And behold, the word of the Lord came to him, saying, this man shall not be your heir, but he who shall come from your own body shall be your heir.

I believe the Lord and it is counted to me for righteousness.

⁶And he [Abram] believed in (trusted in, relied on, remained steadfast to) the Lord, and He counted it to him as righteousness (right standing with God).

My spiritual seed shall be as the stars of heaven.

⁵And He brought him outside [his tent into the starlight] and said, Look now toward the heavens and count the stars—if you are able to number them. Then He said to him, So shall your descendants be.

God brought me out of the past to bring me into my spiritual inheritance.

⁷And He said to him, I am the [same] Lord, Who brought you out of Ur of the Chaldees to give you this land as an inheritance.

God brought me out of the bondage of slavery to sin.

¹³And [God] said to Abram, Know positively that your descendants will be strangers dwelling as temporary residents in a land that is not theirs [Egypt], and they will be slaves there and will be afflicted and oppressed for 400 years.

God will judge those who enslaved me. I will be brought out of every bondage with great spiritual and material substance.

¹⁴But I will bring judgment on that nation whom they will serve, and afterward they will come out with great possessions.

I will join my Godly ancestors in eternity. I will live to accomplish my destiny.

¹⁵And you shall go to your fathers in peace; you shall be buried at a good old (hoary) age.

My seed will be preserved and return to their spiritual roots.

¹⁶And in the fourth generation they [your descendants] shall come back here [to Canaan] again, for the iniquity of the Amorites is not yet full and complete

My seed will inherit their rightful possessions. God has established my spiritual boundaries, and nothing can change them.

¹⁸On the same day the Lord made a covenant (promise, pledge) with Abram, saying, To your descendants I have given this land, from the river of Egypt to the great river Euphrates

My declaration according to Genesis 17:1-22:

This is a supernatural covenant established between God and me.

¹WHEN ABRAM was ninety-nine years old, the Lord appeared to him and said, I am the Almighty God; walk and live habitually before Me and be perfect (blameless, wholehearted, complete).

God will multiply me exceedingly.

²And I will make My covenant (solemn pledge) between Me and you and will multiply you exceedingly.

God's covenant is with me. I will be the spiritual parent of nations.

⁴As for Me, behold, My covenant (solemn pledge) is with you, and you shall be the father of many nations.

God will change my spiritual identity to reflect His purposes.

⁵Nor shall your name any longer be Abram [high, exalted father]; but your name shall be Abraham [father of a multitude], for I have made you the father of many nations.

I will be exceedingly fruitful in every area of life. I will multiply spiritually and affect the destiny of entire nations. I will raise up spiritually great men and women.

⁶And I will make you exceedingly fruitful and I will make nations of you, and kings will come from you.

This covenant is everlasting. God will be God to me. God will be God to my spiritual and material seed.

⁷And I will establish My covenant between Me and you and your descendants after you throughout their generations for an everlasting, solemn pledge, to be a God to you and to your posterity after you.

God will give me my rightful inheritance as an everlasting possession. He will be my seed's God.

⁸And I will give to you and to your posterity after you the land in which you are a stranger [going from place to place], all the land of Canaan, for an everlasting possession; and I will be their God.

This covenant has been sealed by the blood of Jesus Christ.

¹⁹But God said, Sarah your wife shall bear you a son indeed, and you shall call his name Isaac [laughter]; and I will establish My covenant

or solemn pledge with him for an everlasting covenant and with his posterity after him.

<u>Like Sarah, my spiritual identity will be changed and I will become fruitful.</u>

¹⁵And God said to Abraham, As for Sarai your wife, you shall not call her name Sarai; but Sarah [Princess] her name shall be.

<u>God will bless me. He will raise up spiritual sons and daughters to me. I will be the spiritual mentor of nations. I will bring forth strong spiritual leaders.</u>

¹⁶And I will bless her and give you a son also by her. Yes, I will bless her, and she shall be a mother of nations; kings of peoples shall come from her.

<u>My children will be birthed by the Spirit (like Isaac), not of the flesh (like Ishmael). This covenant is established with me forever. This covenant is established with my seed forever.</u>

¹⁹But God said, Sarah your wife shall bear you a son indeed, and you shall call his name Isaac [laughter]; and I will establish My covenant or solemn pledge with him for an everlasting covenant and with his posterity after him.

<u>God will make all related to me spiritually fruitful. God will multiply all related to me spiritually. I will bring forth spiritual heirs. My seed will be a great spiritual nation.</u>

²⁰And as for Ishmael, I have heard and heeded you: behold, I will bless him and will make him fruitful and will multiply him exceedingly; He will be the father of twelve princes, and I will make him a great nation.

<u>God will bless all of my efforts (Ishmael), but His divine covenant comes supernaturally through His Spirit (Isaac).</u>

²¹But My covenant, My promise and pledge, I will establish with Isaac, whom Sarah will bear to you at this season next year.

My declaration according to Genesis 22:16-18 :

God has guaranteed these blessings are mine with His own oath.

¹⁶And said, I have sworn by Myself, says the Lord, that since you have done this and have not withheld [from Me] or begrudged [giving Me] your son, your only son,

God will bless me as I bless others. God will multiply my spiritual seed as the stars and sand. My spiritual seed will possess the gate of the enemy.

¹⁷In blessing I will bless you and in multiplying I will multiply your descendants like the stars of the heavens and like the sand on the seashore. And your Seed (Heir) will possess the gate of His enemies,

My spiritual seed will bless all families (the nations) of the earth.

¹⁸And in your Seed [Christ] shall all the nations of the earth be blessed and [by Him] bless themselves, because you have heard and obeyed My voice.

CONTACT AND BOOKING INFORMATION

ROBIN HEALING MINISTRIES
133-17 101 Avenue, South Ozone Park
New York, 11419

Telephone No: 718-725-1400 / Fax No: 718-725-1401
Web: www.robinhealingministry.com
Email: robind@robinhealingministry.com

Precious gifts cafe book shop

Micah 2:13
Breakers anointing